IT'S TIME:

HEAL YOUR INNER CHILD AND COME BACK HOME

REPROGRAM THE PAST AND MOVE BEYOND FEAR AND TRAUMA TO CULTIVATE HEALTHY RELATIONSHIPS WITH SELF AND OTHERS BY LIVING MORE AUTHENTICALLY

COURTNEY RYAN

CONTENTS

INTRODUCTION

Are you struggling to understand why you find yourself in certain self-sabotaging situations? Is something missing from your life—like an unknown part of yourself needs to be unearthed and nurtured? Or maybe you feel like you're stuck in a cycle of negative thinking and can't seem to break free. If so, then inner child work may be the answer.

Inner child work is an approach that seeks to explore our childhood experiences and unresolved feelings from earlier stages of life. It helps us understand our current patterns of behavior and emotional responses, as well as uncover our authentic selves. By reconnecting with and healing our inner child, we can heal ourselves, give ourselves more self-compassion, and create a better life.

Growing up as a child, I lacked the words or phrases for the experiences I had. As a result, I didn't always feel safe expressing all of my feelings, or I didn't understand why I was feeling the way I was. It was only my mother and me, and I didn't want to burden her with my experiences, either. So, when I was feeling overwhelmed with emotions, I stuffed them away and avoided their message.

My behavior slowly grew worse over the years, but my mother, busy with her work, friends, and life, couldn't really keep up. I think this is when my inner child really rooted within me.

In my adult years, I acted out. While it's normal for teenagers to experiment or act out, I didn't stop when it came time to grow up. I was emotionally numb and couldn't relate to people in a healthy way. Instead, I mistreated people—was mean and aggressive—and thought I had it all figured out. I treated myself poorly, in the same ways I had been treated when I was a child. I constantly recreated the same scenarios in life, searching for love and approval, but never really finding it.

And then one day, I took it too far. I lost my cool at work, toward my boss and colleagues, and I was fired. As I walked home on the frosty night, I thought to myself, *If this is how I'm going to live my life, then what's the point?* I was exhausted and had hit my breaking point. This is when I started to look inward. I faced the truth about myself and the root cause of my behavior to find the courage to start healing myself.

This is how I began my own journey with inner child work, which has since changed my life. Through this journey of inner exploration, I reconnected with the part of me that felt scared, misunderstood, neglected, and forgotten. When I reconnected and healed my inner child, I finally broke free from the cycle of negative thinking and behavior.

I understand that my childhood experiences have shaped me into the person I am today, and this realization has been an extremely powerful source of growth. It has given me the tools and understanding to recognize my triggers and manage my emotions more effectively. It has also helped me become a better person, with more self-awareness and compassion for myself and others.

And now, I want to share those tools and knowledge with you. When my inner child was acting out, I didn't just hurt the people around me—I hurt myself, too. It was only when I began to understand why my inner child was acting out and came to terms with the pain of my past that I could heal and move forward.

That's what this book is for. Over the next several chapters, I will provide an in-depth look at inner child work and how you can use it to heal and create a better life. You'll learn about various techniques, such as visualization and journaling, that can help you unlock your inner child and reconcile with the parts of yourself that have been neglected or forgotten.

Healing your inner child isn't as tough or time-consuming as you may have been led to believe. It requires a commitment to yourself, a desire to learn more about your inner world, and the courage to start making changes in your life. However, you can make these adjustments slowly—and one at a time. Inner child work can be a powerful way to reclaim your life while honoring and respecting who you are.

Since I started working on my inner child, I've noticed a remarkable improvement in my life. Managing my emotions is easier, and I have more meaningful relationships with others. I've developed a greater sense of peace and self-love. My life is no longer unhappy or full of negative thinking and behaviors. I want you to have the same opportunity. Join me in the next chapter and together, let's start exploring your inner world. The journey will be worth it. I promise.

PART 1:

RECONNECTING WITH THE CHILD WITHIN

CHAPTER

1

DON'T UNDERESTIMATE YOUR INNER CHILD

Your inner child is just that—a child. They can be mischievous, curious, vulnerable, and daring. They may also be scared and overwhelmed by the world around them. However, your inner child has needs just like any other person. When we grow up, it's easy to forget about our inner child and ignore them for years. We might think they are silly, immature, or unimportant. But don't underestimate your inner child—they are the powerful source behind your actions and emotions. In this chapter, we will explore why and how inner child work can help you heal and find your power, so you can begin to live a more fulfilled life.

THE REALITY OF THE INNER CHILD

The inner child is a concept that refers to the part of us that remembers how we felt, thought, and acted as children. The inner child is a part of our conscious mind that stores our earliest memories and experiences, from childhood and even before. It holds all the beliefs, emotions, and impressions established during those formative years, which are often still influencing us today. The inner child is an intuitive source of wisdom that knows how to respond to situations based on its past experiences and can differ from the logical adult mind.

Accessing this part of ourselves can be tough, as our adult selves often override it with logic and reason. It requires us to look back into our past and recall moments from when we were younger. In order to do this work properly, it's best to connect with your feelings and emotions on a deeper level.

Identifying our inner child requires us to take a pause and look at ourselves from a more compassionate perspective. By slowing down and being honest with ourselves about what we're feeling in any given situation, we can start to listen to the voice of our inner child. This may present itself as fear, shame, or anger; it may even appear differently on unique occasions.

However, the inner child holds invaluable insight into how we were affected by our early childhood experiences and can provide us with valuable guidance in navigating our current lives. We can make sense of why we behave in certain ways or have certain emotional reactions.

The reality of our inner child is that it is always present and communicating with us, though it may often go unheard or unnoticed. Acknowledging and embracing our inner child allows us to access deeper levels of understanding about ourselves that may have remained hidden or suppressed for years. When we honor this part of ourselves, we can tap into a wealth of information about what makes us who we are and how to become better versions of ourselves.

Healing our inner child involves exploring those feelings and working through the unresolved issues they bring up. Through this journey, we realize the root causes behind unhelpful patterns of behavior or thoughts, allowing us to release them in order to move forward in life. This process also helps us build greater self-awareness and create healthier relationships with others as well as ourselves. Healing allows us to gain insight into what lies behind certain triggers or reactions so that we can respond consciously rather than reacting habitually based on old wounds from the past.

Healing the inner child is more than simply identifying what happened in the past. It's also about understanding how those experiences shaped who you are today and how they continue to affect your life in both positive and negative ways. This process involves self-reflection and self-compassion, so you can come to terms with any unresolved issues or trauma you may have experienced during childhood. Additionally, healing your inner child involves learning how to nurture yourself, providing yourself with comfort and understanding, acknowledging your own needs instead of hiding them away, and being kinder to yourself in general.

Inner child healing is an important process for anyone seeking greater personal growth and development. This practice helps them reconnect with their true selves on an emotional level rather than simply relying on logic or rational thinking. Inner child work enables people to feel empowered within themselves by honoring their core feelings, allowing them to trust in their intuition rather than bury it under layers of doubt or fear instilled by outside influences throughout life.

WHY THE INNER CHILD WORK IS GROWING IN POPULARITY

Inner child work is gaining popularity due to its ability to help people heal from emotional wounds and trauma that may have been experienced during childhood. This type of healing helps people gain insight into their own life experiences, uncovering old habits and patterns that no longer serve them, and ultimately allowing them to move forward in a healthier and more balanced way.

Psychologically speaking, inner child work focuses on reparenting ourselves in order to undo the false beliefs we've developed about ourselves as children. Doing so allows us to take back our power. This could include learning how to trust one's own feelings, emotions, and intuition, rather than internalizing the words or behaviors of others. By bringing awareness to these suppressed or ignored parts of ourselves, we can begin to accept our true selves and embrace our entire being.

Inner child healing can help you explore how your current issues may be rooted in childhood experiences. It can help you develop an understanding of why they have certain behaviors or thought patterns today. It also provides a platform for addressing any unresolved emotions such as guilt, shame, anger, hurt, or fear which can contribute to mental health issues, such as depression or anxiety. By validating the past pain of the inner child through self-compassion, forgiveness, and acceptance, it is possible to find peace within oneself.

The benefits of inner child healing are vast. By engaging with this work, we can improve our overall psychological well-being, including increased self-esteem, improved relationships with others as well as an improved rela-

Like spending time alone - Hiding or processing thoughts

tionship with self. Additionally, it allows us to reclaim control over our lives by providing us with new coping strategies for dealing with stressors that arise in everyday life.

This work also gives us an opportunity for creative growth by breaking free from old limiting patterns that once held us back from reaching our potential. Ultimately, inner child work helps us reconnect with our true essence so that we may live authentically from a place of love rather than fear. This prompts us to become more fully integrated, both spiritually on a soul level and psychologically within the greater collective consciousness.

WHY PEOPLE UNDERESTIMATED THE IMPORTANCE OF THE INNER CHILD

Over the years, people underestimated the importance of the inner child because it was traditionally viewed as "foolishness" or a "hocus pocus" process that lacked any true scientific merit and credibility. There was a stigma attached to the concept of an inner child and healing processes, which made many people skeptical about their potential effectiveness. People didn't believe in the inner child because they felt it focused on something that could not be seen, touched, or measured. This skepticism and doubt caused them to think negatively about the healing process and its potential benefits.

In addition, many people also don't believe in the existence of an "inner child." People saw the inner child as a figment of our imagination rather than an actual part of ourselves that requires attention and healing. This mindset can make us forget that we all have an unconscious mind, filled with forgotten memories and experiences from our past that still influence us today. However, as children, we often have difficulty expressing or understanding our emotions. As a result, these unresolved feelings end up lodged deeply within us and remain unaddressed until adulthood if they are not properly processed and healed.

This stigma about our inner child can be traced back to a deep-rooted cultural belief that one should not focus on one's emotions, but rather suppress them in order to achieve success in life. People believed that healing was a sign of weakness, as it showed that someone could not cope with their issues by themselves. This stigma surrounding inner child healing processes has caused many people to underestimate its importance and even ridicule those who practice it.

worried
people don't
like me

The idea that our minds can be hurt by childhood experiences was considered too abstract for many people to comprehend or even accept. People often thought that the emotions associated with the inner child were just a result of overthinking and reflection, rather than valid feelings generated early in life. As a result, they tended to ignore their own childhood memories and associated feelings as being unimportant. In addition, some individuals considered themselves too old or mature to bother dealing with such issues from long ago and preferred burying them instead of confronting them head-on.

There were also those who believed that one shouldn't have to go through this type of therapy if one is already an adult. After all, adults should have already moved past their childhood traumas by then. There are still some people who think that focusing on our inner child is simply another way for someone to make money off vulnerable individuals looking for ways to cope with life's difficulties. Even though these beliefs are misguided, they still, unfortunately, exist today, causing many people to look down upon inner child work and other healing processes related to it.

HOW A HEALTHY AND HAPPY INNER CHILD CAN TURN OUR LIVES AROUND

While there is still some stigma surrounding inner child healing, the concept of inner child work is gaining traction in recent years as more people are recognizing the importance of addressing their inner wounds from childhood and how it can affect us as adults. Healing our inner child is key to creating a healthy, balanced, and happy life. Some say that if we want to be truly successful in life, we must first learn how to nurture ourselves and reconnect with our inner child.

When we think about our inner child, it may bring up hard memories and emotions. This is normal; however, by bringing awareness to these feelings, we can heal them and move forward in life with a sense of peace and acceptance. By connecting with our inner child, we can start to recognize patterns that no longer serve us and begin to break free from them. Inner healing helps us understand the root cause of our suffering so that we can start making better choices for ourselves.

Getting to know your inner child allows you to release any negative beliefs or thought patterns that have been holding you back since childhood. Through this process of self-exploration, you can gain insight into what triggers certain behaviors in yourself or others. You will also gain an understanding of why certain aspects of life have been challenging for you or why you may struggle with certain aspects now—allowing for healing on the deepest levels possible.

One major benefit of healing your inner child is increased self-awareness and greater self-love and acceptance. As adults, many times we look at our childhoods through rose-colored glasses. However, by looking back at our younger selves compassionately through the lens of an adult, we can gain perspective on how these early experiences shaped us into who we are today. Then we can make conscious decisions to steer away from some negative patterns while embracing the positive elements instead.

In addition, by reconnecting with your inner child, you become more empathetic toward yourself as well as toward others. This will lead to forming deeper connections with those around you. Finally, once healed, your newfound understanding will allow you to manifest positive changes in all areas of your life—from relationships, career paths, and financial situations—to simply having a better overall outlook on life and feeling more contentment within yourself.

MYTHS ABOUT THE INNER CHILD THAT YOU NEED TO DISCARD NOW

As we discussed above, people still have certain beliefs or stigmas around inner child work. These myths can be damaging, so it's important to dispel them. Below are some of the most common myths people have about inner child work you need to discard now.

- Myth: The inner child is only a product of the imagination.

Fact: While it may feel imaginary at times, the inner child is very real. This aspect of ourselves is a representation of our unresolved early life experiences and emotions that are held within us. Working with the inner child can help bring awareness to these issues and ultimately help us heal them.

- Myth: The healing process requires you to fully recover all childhood memories in order to heal your inner child.

Fact: It's unnecessary to remember all of your childhood memories to heal efficiently. In fact, some memories can be too overwhelming or painful to revisit and this could impede your healing process rather than aid it. Instead, focus on being present with yourself in the moment, allowing any feelings or thoughts to come up as they do without judging them, and simply observe how they make you feel. This will create more space for understanding and healing those aspects that need attention and care now, without forcing yourself into remembering everything from childhood.

- Myth: Inner child work is only for adults who experienced traumatic childhoods.

Fact: Inner child work is beneficial for anyone going through any type of difficulty, regardless of if their childhood was traumatic. Experience has shown that when we learn how to understand our inner child's needs, we can better cope with adult challenges such as stress, anxiety, depression, and even physical illness by gaining insight into our underlying emotions which are often rooted in our past as children or adolescents.

- Myth: Inner child work will solve all of my problems overnight!

Fact: Inner Child Work is an ongoing process that requires dedication in order to see results over time. You may experience brief moments of relief due to a deeper understanding of yourself. However, true transformation takes consistency and patience over an extended period of time. It's like planting a tree—you have to water it daily before you will see any fruit grow on its branches!

- Myth: You need a therapist to heal your inner child.

Fact: While there may be valuable benefits to seeking out therapy or counseling when healing your inner child, many people can do this work on their own with patience and commitment. Inner child work requires us to go deep within ourselves without judgment and take responsibility for our emotions.

- Myth: Once I've healed my inner child, I won't ever face difficulties again

Fact: While there are many positive outcomes associated with healing the inner child, including increased self-awareness, improved self-esteem, enhanced relationships, etc., challenges will still arise throughout life. However, having gone through this process, one should be better equipped with greater emotional resilience due to having developed healthier coping strategies. In addition, working through difficult times becomes easier since connecting back to our core wound allows us access to knowledge about ourselves that aids in moving forward gracefully.

- Myth: It takes years for me to heal my inner child.

Fact: Healing does not have a timeline attached, so one should not place expectations of themselves about when one should complete their journey. Rather, one should take their time because it usually varies from person-to-person depending on several factors, such as individual history, level of commitment, and motivation levels, among other things. What matters most is creating space for oneself while showing compassion throughout the entire journey so that healing happens naturally, eventually leading toward integration within oneself.

- Myth: Once I heal my inner child, I won't have any negative emotions anymore.

Fact: Emotions are part of being human. Therefore, even after someone goes through their entire internal healing journey, expectations should not be placed upon themselves to experience perfect days free from difficulty or even negative emotionality. Instead, newly gained emotional regulation skills stemming from reconnecting with their authentic selves will serve them best in managing whatever arises. Then they can recognize what they need at any given moment rather than reacting impulsively, thus bringing about greater balance and peace within themselves over time.

- Myth: Healing means forgetting about my past trauma or difficulties altogether.

Fact: Healing doesn't mean forgetting, but rather remembering differently such that one holds onto lessons learned instead of being overwhelmed by unresolved pain linked with traumatic events from the past. This allows us to acknowledge what happened without carrying around baggage. This in turn prevents similar patterns from reoccurring down the line while making sure we create boundaries and enforce them if needed. Then we don't end up repeating dysfunctional cycles created during earlier stages in life due to a lack of self-awareness and understanding about oneself at those given periods.

- Myth: It's too late for me now—I waited too long already!

Fact: No matter how long ago something happened or how much time has passed since then, it's never too late!

- Myth: It's impossible to reclaim lost childhood experiences.

Fact: The beauty of doing inner child work is that one can reclaim some lost pieces, experiences, or memories, even if they think nothing remains of it anymore. Although memories fade away over time due to repressing them within oneself, they are still imprinted onto one's soul and by paying attention closely inside oneself. You can tend those marks back into new life thus reclaiming parts which once thought lost forever.

- Myth: You need to have an open relationship with your parents for inner child work to be successful.

Fact: Although having an open relationship with one's parents could surely help expedite the process toward successful inner child healing, it also isn't necessary at all. This kind of work takes place solely within oneself regardless of external circumstances or relationships thus implying complete autonomy over one's journey back home toward one's true self.

- Myth: It takes too much time and effort to do inner child work.

Fact: Contrary to popular belief, completing an effective session of inner child work doesn't actually take up too much time or too much effort. This healing process is mainly about slowing down long enough so that one can deeply connect with their core essence while taking gradual steps toward releasing any unresolved trauma surrounding areas where deeper understanding and compassionate acceptance are sorely needed.

CHAPTER

2

FINDING RELEASE FROM TRAUMA

n the last chapter, we reviewed why our inner child is so important and how they are connected to our actions and emotions. Our unresolved hurt, pain, and trauma from childhood can have a lasting impact on us as adults. This is where inner child work comes in. Through inner child work, we can explore these unresolved emotions, learn to identify them, and find ways to heal from the traumatic experiences of our past. By releasing ourselves from the trauma of our past, we can start to find new ways to express ourselves and discover our true, authentic selves.

IS DIGGING UP THE PAST HELPFUL OR HARMFUL?

Digging up the past can be both helpful and harmful. While it is important to process unresolved hurts, analyze the past, and reconnect with our inner child in order to heal, we must also take care to recognize our own emotional limits and boundaries.

Healing the inner child involves recognizing and understanding the feelings of hurt that were created by experiences or relationships. This often requires reflecting on our own upbringing, family dynamics, or other relationships that may have left wounds that need healing. It is important to be honest with ourselves about the hurt we experienced in the past so that we can begin the process of healing it.

Analyzing and understanding why certain events or interactions occurred can be a crucial part of healing from unresolved hurts. Understanding how our experiences shaped us allows us to grow and move on from them in healthier ways. We can also learn how to better respond in similar situations going forward.

However, it is important to remember that not all emotions are healthy for us to dwell on indefinitely. Sometimes ruminating on past experiences can cause more harm than good. It is essential for us to recognize when we have reached a point where further reflection is no longer productive and instead causes more pain or stress than before. As such, digging up the past should always be done with caution and self-awareness. If it begins causing more distress than closure, then it may be time to give ourselves some space from those memories. Instead, you can still work on healing through different methods, such as therapy or journaling.

In conclusion, digging up the past can be a helpful part of healing unresolved hurts, but must always be done with caution and respect for our own individual emotional limits. However, sometimes further reflection simply isn't beneficial anymore. If so, taking a break from delving into these memories may prove necessary until we can approach them again in a healthier way.

WHAT CAUSES A WOUNDED INNER CHILD?

A wounded inner child is the manifestation of unresolved childhood trauma that has not been properly addressed. This trauma can be caused by a variety of sources, such as physical, psychological, or emotional abuse. Other traumas can include neglect, violence, illness, or the death of a parent or loved one. The child's inner world is then filled with hurt, fear, confusion, and pain. Over time, these unresolved wounds become buried deep within the subconscious mind and are hidden from conscious awareness.

The wounds that the inner child carries can vary depending on the underlying source of the trauma and its severity. For example, physical abuse or neglect can lead to feelings of insecurity and vulnerability, while emotional abuse can cause feelings of low self-esteem, shame, guilt, and self-hatred. Psychological trauma can lead to more complex responses, such as difficulty trusting others or engaging in relationships, distorted views of reality, maladaptive coping strategies (e.g., substance use), or relationship difficulties.

The scars that remain from a wounded inner child are often deep and long-lasting. They can manifest in various ways throughout adulthood. As an adult attempts to cope with their unresolved pain from childhood, they may turn to unhealthy or destructive ways, such as avoiding relationships or turning to alcohol or drugs for solace. Besides this outward behavior, an individual may also experience psychological impacts such as flashbacks to earlier traumatic events, intense negative emotions, like fear and anger, that are difficult to manage or control, or distorted beliefs about oneself.

Additionally, other common scars are intrusive thoughts about past traumas, difficulty forming intimate relationships due to trust issues, difficulty connecting emotionally with others due to feeling unworthy of love, connection, or happiness, feeling disconnected from one's own body because of numbness or dissociation—just to name a few!

The effects of a wounded inner child can be debilitating if they go unaddressed. However, with proper understanding and treatment, they can be healed over time. This allows individuals to reclaim their true selves beneath any false beliefs they may have created over time in order to cope with their hurt feelings from childhood trauma. By understanding what causes a wounded inner child—i.e., unresolved childhood trauma—individuals can assess themselves for these unresolved hurts. Then they can begin healing themselves in order to live healthier lives without being weighed down by the false self-created out of pain and suffering from long-ago experiences.

Signs Your Inner Child is Still Hurt

There are several signs that your inner child is still hurt. These can include an inability to trust, feelings of worthlessness and self-doubt, and a fear of abandonment or rejection from others. Chronic anger and resentment toward yourself or others, difficulty forming and maintaining relationships, compulsive behaviors like overworking or overspending, issues with authority figures, and difficulty finding joy or fulfillment in life are also other common signs that your inner child might be hurt.

These signs may manifest in different ways, depending on the person. For example, someone who has unresolved hurts may become withdrawn and isolated from friends and family. They may spend more time alone than they used to in order to avoid any possible harmful interactions. This person may also have a hard time expressing their authentic emotions and might bottle them up or push them away. They may also be extremely critical of themselves and find it difficult to accept compliments or positive feedback from others.

Besides this psychological withdrawal, unresolved hurts can affect physical health as well. A person who is struggling with past trauma may experience chronic pain, which could be because of the physical tension caused by holding onto the pain. Other physical symptoms, such as fatigue, headaches, stomach problems, insomnia, palpitations, and skin problems, could also indicate that the inner child is still hurting.

The inner child will often act out these unresolved feelings in a variety of ways. For example, someone who has been hurt in the past may be prone to sudden tantrums and outbursts when feeling overwhelmed by emotions or stressors that trigger those past traumas. They might also engage in self-sabotaging behaviors like extreme risk-taking or substance abuse as a way of numbing their emotional pain without realizing the actual root cause of the issue. Sometimes, they might even resort to self-harm as a means of expression for their repressed emotions when other methods are ineffective at releasing those built-up feelings within oneself.

When assessing whether your inner child is still hurting, it's important to pay attention not only to your mental state but also to your body's reactions to certain stimuli that trigger old wounds. These triggers could cause physical tension or discomfort and emotional distress. If you find yourself overwhelmed by these responses, it might be helpful to reach out for professional help. Learning how to cope with your unresolved hurts in healthier ways while reconnecting with your inner child and letting go of the false self you created because of them is crucial to healing effectively.

LETTING GO OF YOUR FALSE SELF

The False Self is a defense mechanism created by the individual to protect themselves from feeling pain, anger, or resentment. It involves masking one's true feelings and presenting an artificial version of oneself in order to please or appease others. In extreme cases, it can lead to a sense of being "dead" on the inside and may even cause depression or anxiety.

What Are Different False Selves?

When it comes to false selves, there are five distinct patterns identified by renowned psychoanalyst Donald Winnicott: leaving pattern, merging pattern, enduring pattern, aggressive pattern, and rigid pattern (*Letting Go of the False Self,* 2019). Each of these can be further broken down into more specific behaviors.

The leaving pattern involves withdrawing from relationships or situations that make us feel uncomfortable. We try to avoid any kind of emotional confrontation by keeping our distance from people and situations that could potentially cause us harm.

The merging pattern is when we try to blend in with other people so as not to stand out. We try to conform our behavior and tastes to what we think will be accepted by the group we are trying to fit in with.

The enduring pattern is when we stay in a situation, even though it makes us feel uncomfortable because we would rather endure than risk the uncertainty of change. This can include staying in unsatisfying relationships and dealing with difficult work environments.

The aggressive pattern is when people act out their frustrations through anger and violence directed toward those around them rather than addressing the core issue itself.

Finally, there is the rigid pattern, which occurs when someone tries desperately hard not to break any rules or conventions for fear of rejection or punishment. People who use this type of coping mechanism often struggle with making decisions that could go against societal expectations or norms.

By recognizing our false selves, we can begin to address how they manifest in our lives. This will allow us to determine which steps to take toward letting them go. Then we can move closer toward living an authentic life rooted in our true selves where we no longer need protection from pain or fear but can instead embrace vulnerability as part of being alive and human.

RECONNECTING WITH YOUR INNER CHILD: WHAT WORKS?

Reconnecting with your inner child is an important part of healing the wounds of the past and developing a healthier, more positive relationship with yourself. It can help you understand yourself better and to feel more connected to your emotions, which leads to greater acceptance and joy in life.

Journaling is a great way to reconnect with your inner child. Writing down your thoughts, feelings, and experiences can help you identify patterns in your emotions that may have gone unnoticed before. You can also write letters to your inner child, expressing love and forgiveness, or simply letting them know that they are heard and valued.

Inner child visualization is another amazing tool for reconnecting with your inner child. Visualize them as a youthful version of yourself surrounded by love and safety. Imagine talking with them or comforting them when they're scared or hurt. This exercise can help you get in touch with what they need emotionally so that you can provide it for yourself today.

Affirmations are another powerful way to heal any unresolved issues from childhood or adolescence. Identify the areas where you struggle most (i.e., self-worth, anxiety, or depression) and create an affirmation specifically for that area of struggle. For instance, you can tell yourself "I am worthy" or "I am safe" and repeat it often throughout the day until it becomes ingrained in your brain on a subconscious level.

Mindfulness and meditation can also be helpful for connecting with our inner child selves by allowing us to get in touch with our true feelings without judgment or criticism. Take time each day to just sit still and observe your thoughts without trying to change them or make them go away; this will help you become aware of any repressed emotions that may still linger inside of you from years gone by.

Unresolved issues from our childhoods can manifest themselves in many ways throughout our lives, but healing these issues starts within ourselves by reconnecting with our inner children through journaling, writing letters, visualizing, affirmations, mindfulness, and meditation exercises so we can learn how best to give ourselves the love we need right now.

Staying Connected to Your Inner Child

Connecting to your inner child can bring about many positive benefits in your life. By taking the steps to re-engage with your inner child, you can experience a greater sense of joy and vitality in your life. Taking the time to reconnect with your inner child allows you to access a deeper level of self-knowledge and understanding that can be immensely beneficial for personal growth. Not only does staying connected to your inner child provide an opportunity for self-discovery, but it also helps reduce stress and anxiety levels by helping you stay grounded and centered in present moments.

One great way to stay connected to your inner child is by living more in the moment and being mindful of what's happening around you. Being mindful allows you to consciously observe the little details of everyday life that can easily go unnoticed when we're too caught up in our own thoughts or worries. By taking more time out of our day to appreciate what's going on around us, we can tap into our curiosity, which was once so prevalent when we were children. This curiosity will allow us to go on fresh adventures and explore new ideas that may otherwise have been overlooked due to our adult responsibilities or worries.

Another way to connect with your inner child is by being more honest with yourself about how you really feel about situations or people in your life. As adults, we often pretend like everything is okay, even when it isn't. We do this because we don't want others to think poorly of us or question why things are like they are. But by being honest with yourself, it allows you to express yourself authentically and find out what truly matters most deep down inside—a task that was much easier for us as children before societal expectations took hold of us.

Taking risks can also be a powerful way to stay connected with your inner child as it encourages exploration and growth. However, this is something we tend not to worry about as much as adults due to a lack of security or fear of failure. When taking risks, it's important not just to focus on the outcome but rather accept the journey itself, knowing that whatever happens will bring knowledge and experience no matter if it fails or succeeds. Alongside taking risks, having trust in yourself is key to maintaining a connection with your inner child. Trust gives us the courage to take action on new opportunities without fear guiding our decisions instead.

Lastly, going outside and playing can help ground you back into childhood innocence while helping relieve stress at the same time. Other activities that promote creativity such as drawing, and writing stories or songs are also wonderful ways of reconnecting with our inner selves. These activities will help with expressing emotions that may otherwise remain unspoken due to societal pressures put upon ourselves as adults.

Additionally, appreciating nature through hikes or camping trips can allow us to gain insight into how small each one of us truly is within this immense world. This understanding is something that often gets muddled when growing up surrounded by modern society's norms and expectations but is incredibly sobering.

Overall, by staying connected to your inner being, you can attain greater clarity of who you really are and also enjoy life more fully. You can have genuine joy within yourself rather than seeking external sources for validation every single time.

INNER CHILD HEALING WORKSHEETS

Describe your inner child: Take a moment to consider what your inner child looks like. How old are they? When you envision them, do they have an expression? If so, which expression do they portray? How are they feeling? Are they angry? Stressed? Anxious? Or lonely? Don't worry about spelling or grammar, simply allow your feelings to pour out of you.

What is the inner child's story? Take the time to write your inner child's story, focusing on the parts that stand out to you and need to be explored further. What experiences have shaped them? What struggles have they faced? How can you help them heal?

Discover your inner child's beliefs—reflect on the beliefs your inner child has about themselves and the world around them. What do they believe are their strengths and weaknesses? How does their perception of the world affect their behavior and attitude? Think of a moment from your childhood when you may have felt neglected, hurt, or unsupported, and how this may have influenced your beliefs.

To further evaluate your inner child's beliefs, think about a time you felt hurt, neglected, or unsupported. Record how you felt in the moment and what thoughts were running through your mind. What was the situation? Describe the context and events that took place. Consider what your parents would have said to you. For instance, would they say, "You're a failure," or would they try to instill fear by saying "What until mom or dad gets home"?

Now reflect on your parents' relationship and the emotions they often displayed toward each other. Did they argue often? Or did they show love and compassion toward one another? After you finish this reflection, try to identify any patterns of behavior or emotional responses that your inner child has grown accustomed to having. Is there fear or anger that comes up when certain subjects are discussed?

What are your inner child's dreams? Take a moment to consider what your inner child's goals and ambitions are. Are they dreams of the future? Or hopes of who you could become if given the opportunity? What kind of person do they wish to be? What do they hope to achieve? Reflect on this and write down any ideas that come to mind.

As a child, who were your role models and why? Are they still the same today? Who did you look up to and why? How did they shape your view of the world and what values you uphold? Reflect on this and create a list of the qualities you admire in people and aspire to embody yourself.

Reflect on your earliest memories. What memories come to mind? Are they happy, sad, or neutral? What lessons can you learn from these memories? How have they shaped who you are today?

What was the most grueling experience you faced as a child and how did it affect you? How did this experience shape your beliefs and values? How did it affect the way you view the world? What lessons did this experience give you?

CHAPTER

3

TRUST, LOVE, AND PLAY AGAIN

Now that you understand the causes of your inner child's wounds and how to identify how your inner child's wounds manifest themselves in your life, it's time to discover how to heal those wounds. We reviewed a few options, such as journaling or practicing mindfulness. However, in this chapter, we will focus on how to deepen and solidify your bond with your inner child.

We'll delve deeper into inner child work and how you can use it to create a healthier relationship with yourself and your inner child. Inner child work is all about creating a safe environment where you can be vulnerable, open, and honest with yourself. You'll learn how to express your deepest emotions while developing trust in yourself so that you can take care of your inner child.

WHAT CAN WE LEARN BY OBSERVING A CHILD'S CAREFREE SPIRIT?

When observing a child's carefree spirit, it's hard not to be inspired by how they approach life. Children have an inner belief that nothing is impossible and their enthusiasm for life can help us become more conscious of the potential of what we can achieve. By observing a child's carefree spirit, we can learn how to foster a sense of trust and faith in ourselves and others.

A child's joy often comes from the simple act of laughing, whether it be at themselves or with others. We can learn to be less hard on ourselves when something goes wrong and instead focus on finding the humor in everyday situations. Asking silly questions allows children to explore the world around them with no preconceived notions or expectations. This inquisitive nature gives us permission to access our inner curiosities fearlessly, allowing us to discover new perspectives and possibilities.

At times, children may experience disappointment or hurt feelings from not getting their way or being told "no." Being witness to this provides us an opportunity to cultivate more compassion within ourselves as well as toward others who are going through difficult moments in life. It reminds us that everyone has moments when they feel downhearted and those are just as deserving of attention and comfort as joyous moments.

We can also learn from children how to start each day with fresh eyes. They don't carry grudges from yesterday but look forward with excitement and anticipation for what lies ahead. Adopting this mindset can give us a much-needed break from habitually thinking about worries or trying to out-do ourselves every day.

On a deeper level, embodying a child's carefree spirit helps bring out our own inner playful energy. This allows us to be uninhibited and free while still being mindful of our environment and relationships around us—and respecting boundaries. Instead of trying to overanalyze a situation or feeling pressure to achieve certain goals, we can take on the beginner's mindset that children possess. We can enjoy each moment for what it is and appreciate the process instead of focusing solely on results.

Dreams are another thing that comes naturally for children. Their imaginations run wild with ideas that adults too often shut down due to practicality or because it doesn't fit into society's template of success, accomplishment, or happiness. By observing a child's carefree spirit, we can ignite our own dreams again—believing anything is possible—if only we let ourselves dream without limitations like a child does.

Finally, there is enchantment; something so magical about seeing the world through children's eyes. Noticing beauty where many adults no longer bother looking really allows us all to remember what it feels like when things fill you with joy simply because they exist; helping restore our sense of wonderment which is so often lost as an adult!

THE INNER CHILD AND TRUST ISSUES

Trust issues are complex, but typically arise from a lack of trust in oneself or in others. Trust is the foundation for healthy relationships, so it's important to understand where trust issues come from and how to address them.

In psychology, trust issues may be rooted in our childhood, when we might've felt betrayed, neglected, abandoned, or rejected by someone we loved. This feeling of betrayal can be carried into adulthood and manifest as an inability to trust others. Additionally, unresolved emotional trauma can lead to distrustful beliefs toward oneself and others, causing a person to become suspicious or defensive in relationships.

Common beliefs that contribute to trust issues include: we must be perfect to be accepted; no one will understand me; I can't get hurt again. Other beliefs also include, *I have to take care of myself; I don't deserve love; it's unsafe to let people know my true self;* and *I have no control over my life or feelings.* These underlying beliefs prevent a person from being vulnerable and forming close connections with others.

Several types of trust issues can affect a person's ability to form relationships. Insecurity is a feeling of uncertainty about oneself or one's environment which leads to fear-based thoughts. An individual may feel insecure if they doubt their own worth and capabilities, leading them to be overly suspicious of the intentions and actions of others. Abusive experiences such as violence or neglect can also lead a person to become distrustful of others due to fear of further harm.

Fear of abandonment is another type of trust issue that causes individuals to become preoccupied with the possibility that someone they care about will leave them. Those who experienced emotional neglect or abandonment during childhood often struggle with this type of mistrust. This leads them to not only be afraid of being alone but also too scared and guarded against forming close attachments with anyone else.

Finally, codependency is defined as an unhealthy reliance on other people for approval and validation which can prevent individuals from developing healthy relationships with themselves and others. Codependency occurs when people have difficulty trusting their own instincts and judgment because they rely too heavily on external sources for acceptance and validation. This can lead them to engage in unhealthy behaviors such as clinging onto needy companionship or sacrificing their own needs for another person's approval, happiness, or validation.

The Power of Trusting and Loving Yourself First

Trusting and loving yourself first means having faith in your decisions, beliefs, attitudes, and choices. It is the act of believing in yourself and taking care of your own well-being above all else. Self-trust also involves having a strong sense of self-worth and confidence in who you are and what you stand for.

Signs that you lack self-trust can range from feeling constantly insecure about your decisions to not being able to express yourself openly and honestly. Other signs include struggling to make decisions or speak up when it is needed, difficulty setting boundaries, or feeling like you cannot truly be yourself around others. You may find yourself seeking validation from external sources or overthinking every single move you make. Constantly second-guessing yourself can be a sign of low self-confidence, as well as feelings of unworthiness or inadequacy.

When we do not trust ourselves enough, our minds become filled with negative thoughts that can derail our progress toward achieving goals or reaching our full potential. Fear of failure can cloud our judgment and lead us away from taking risks that could potentially yield positive results. A lack of self-trust can often cause us to doubt our abilities and make us more likely to give up when challenges arise instead of seeing them as opportunities for growth. We may reach out for approval from other people rather than relying on our own instincts, which only serves to further erode our belief in ourselves.

Having faith in oneself allows us to feel empowered knowing that we have everything we need within ourselves to succeed in life; it helps build resilience during difficult times and enables us to create meaningful relationships with the world around us. Building a firm foundation of self-trust allows us to remain true to ourselves no matter what comes our way, which is an essential part of living a fulfilling life filled with purpose, excitement, and joy!

How to Build Self-Trust

Building self-trust is an essential part of learning to love ourselves, as trust allows us to be more open and vulnerable with ourselves. To develop this confidence in ourselves, it is important to listen to our own thoughts and feelings. This will allow us the space to make mistakes and acknowledge the lessons they can teach us.

If you struggle with certain emotions or mistakes, it is important to extend yourself compassion and forgiveness, being gentle when judging your choices. It is also important to understand what boundaries are necessary for your safety, both mentally and physically, and reinforce them when needed. Expressing yourself authentically is also vital for building self-trust. This prompts us to be more honest about who we are and how we feel without fear of judgment from others.

Taking the time to know your values and beliefs will also help create a foundation of trust within yourself, giving you something reliable on which you can rely on no matter what happens. Finally, having a practice that helps bring awareness back inside such as journaling or meditation can help increase self-trust by connecting us more deeply with our inner world. All these practices contribute toward a deeper level of trust in ourselves so that ultimately, we can truly love and accept ourselves just as we are.

Self-Esteem

Self-esteem is an important concept in psychology that refers to how we perceive our worth and value. It is the opinion or belief in ourselves that drives many of the decisions we make throughout life. Self-esteem can be seen as a measure of how much we respect and accept ourselves, and it influences our thoughts, feelings, and behaviors. A person with higher self-esteem feels more confident and secure in their own abilities, while someone with low self-esteem may struggle with feeling inadequate or unworthy.

The importance of self-esteem lies in its ability to shape our behavior and outlook on life. People with high self-esteem often have more successful relationships, better-coping skills during difficult times, and higher academic performance. They often experience less anxiety, have greater resilience when faced with adversity, increased motivation to pursue goals, and think more positively about themselves and life.

On the other hand, people with low self-esteem are more likely to experience depression, anxiety disorders, relationship difficulties, and poor health habits such as smoking or unhealthy eating habits. Low self-esteem can also lead to feelings of inferiority and insecurity which can have a major detrimental effect on overall well-being.

Improving one's self-esteem requires a combination of internal work (self-reflection) and external support (healthy relationships). To improve your self-esteem, you should start by becoming aware of your thought patterns—what do you tend to tell yourself? Are they negative or positive? Once you become conscious of these thoughts, then take steps to replace any negative thoughts with positive ones.

For example, if you find yourself thinking *I am not good enough* then consciously replace this thought within moments with something like *I can achieve any goal I desire* or *I am worthy of accomplishing my dreams*. You can also practice activities such as mindfulness exercises which will help you become more aware of the present moment rather than ruminating over past events or worrying about the future. Additionally, engaging in activities that bring joy into your life such as hobbies or creative outlets can help you gain more appreciation for your own abilities and talents over time.

Recognizing our inner critic is an important step toward improving our self-esteem because it helps us recognize when our thoughts might be overly harsh or critical toward ourselves. We all have moments when we think negatively about ourselves, but it is important not to get stuck in those thought patterns. Instead, you can challenge them by reframing them into something kinder toward yourself.

We all make mistakes, but it is essential that we do not allow these mistakes to define who we are as a person. Instead, we can use them as learning experiences that will help us grow both personally and professionally going forward. When recognizing your inner critic, it is imperative that instead of allowing negative thoughts to linger, you instead choose to reframe them into something productive. You can do this by identifying areas where improvements can be made so that you can hone those skills further over time.

WAYS TO AWAKEN YOUR INNER CHILD'S PLAYFUL SIDE

No matter how old you are, there is an inner child in all of us that just wants to be free and have fun. To awaken this playful side of your inner child, it's important to embrace the spirit of playfulness and trust yourself to take a risk and try something new. Trusting your own instincts is key to unlocking the joys of playing and having fun with others. Whether it's trying a new activity or connecting with someone on an emotional level, trusting that you can do it will help bring out the playful part of yourself.

Love is also an integral part of reawakening your inner child. When we open up our hearts to give and receive love, we create strong relationships with those around us. You can nurture yourself by doing activities that make you feel good or giving compliments to strangers. These acts of kindness will fill your heart with joy and cultivate a sense of self-love that will help you strengthen your relationship with your inner child.

Engaging in activities that bring out the fun-loving nature of your inner child will help unleash its spirit. Join a local recreation center team or find your favorite childhood game from when you were growing up—this could be anything from tag to hide-and-seek! Or find something new to try like learning a language, outdoor sport, or art class. These experiences as an adult can help spark creativity, confidence, and a connection with your youthful side.

Spending time around children can bring about nostalgia for childhood itself, which can be just what's needed to awaken our inner child's sense of wonderment and delight in life again. Making friends who are younger than us can also provide insights into what life was like before adulthood responsibilities took over our lives—it's almost like taking a mini break from reality.

It's also important to look at the world through the eyes of a child. Let yourself admire beauty in things like clouds or sunsets, play music as loud as possible, dance without worrying about what others think, and be silly without fear. There is no wrong way to explore the world—so let yourself feel true freedom while embracing joyous moments along the way!

Finally, express yourself through creativity. You can draw colorful pictures, write poetry or stories, design clothes, cook some new recipes, and take photos or videos. Any type of creative expression helps deepen connections between ourselves and our surroundings while stimulating different parts of our minds at once.

It may feel strange at first but practicing these steps regularly will tap into dormant parts within ourselves that yearn for connection. Then we can embrace trust, love, and play again like we did when we were young.

Working on Your Creativity

Working on your creativity can be a hard task for many people. Creative work tends to require us to dig deep into our inner thoughts and feelings and express them in new ways through whatever medium we choose to use. To help open up this creative pathway, it is important to trust, love, and play again—in other words, let your inner child teach you.

When it comes to trusting yourself, you must learn how to believe in the power of your own ideas. It is easy to criticize yourself or get lost in anxieties about being successful; however, when you give yourself the freedom to imagine without judgment or fear of failure, you often find that the best ideas come from within.

Loving yourself also plays an important role in creativity. If you don't feel connected with yourself or comfortable with who you are, then it is hard to let go of your inhibitions and let creativity take over. Learning how to be kind toward yourself allows for more meaningful self-reflection and greater acceptance of ideas that may not fit within mainstream conventions.

Finally, playing again helps strengthen the bond between creativity and inner peace. When we allow ourselves time for free play, we are reminded of the importance of relaxation and joy in our lives. Not only does this revive our creative spirit, but it also reduces stress which can be helpful when trying to tackle creative tasks.

Allowing your inner child—and their accompanying sense of trust, love, and play—to lead your life can be a powerful tool for anyone looking to reignite their creative spark. Taking the time needed to practice these mindful activities can help open up new avenues for inspiration that can lead to both personal growth and tangible projects filled with passion and enthusiasm.

YOLO: The Good Side

You've likely heard of the saying, "you only live once," aka YOLO. With YOLO, many people think of it as an excuse for taking risks and acting out. However, if used correctly, YOLO can be a great way to reawaken and heal the inner child within all of us. By following the principle of YOLO, we are encouraged to take risks and explore life's possibilities with a renewed sense of joy. This can lead to experiences that potentially bring more meaning into our lives while providing us with opportunities to connect with ourselves on a deeper level.

By embracing YOLO as a guiding principle in our lives, we can make the most out of every experience that comes our way. This is especially true when faced with difficult situations or challenging life events. Following the mantra of "you only live once" provides us with an opportunity to learn from our experiences rather than reacting out of fear or sadness. One example is post-traumatic growth (PTG), which has been identified as the process of positive psychological change after experiencing traumatic or stressful life events. PTG is based on the idea that growth is possible even in the face of difficulty. By embracing a YOLO attitude, you open yourself up for potential growth opportunities that help you gain new insights about yourself and your environment.

Applying a selective approach when engaging in activities can lead to greater satisfaction in life. This concept is known as socioemotional selectivity theory (SST), which suggests that as people age, they become more attuned to their current emotional needs. This causes them to focus more on activities that have immediate benefits such as connecting with friends and family or pursuing meaningful goals. By looking at life through a YOLO lens, we can identify those activities that truly fulfill us now rather than waiting for tomorrow or living in regret due to lack of action today.

LETTING YOUR INNER CHILD HOLD THE REINS FOR ONCE

Letting your inner child hold the reins for once and rediscover your childlike wonder can be an incredibly rewarding experience. Taking the time to enjoy the world around us with fresh eyes can bring us a unique joy that is often missing when we get bogged down in our everyday routines. To do this, it's important to try to step away from our usual point of view and see life through someone else's perspective. We should use all of our senses while engaging with the world, taking in the sights, sounds, smells, tastes, and textures around us. This will help us reconnect with our inner child and can help us really appreciate even the smallest details in life.

It's also important to be spontaneous when engaging with the world around you; try something new or take a different route home from work or school. You never know what you might discover! You could even pick up a passion such as painting, music, or sports to explore your creativity and put yourself into a "flow state" that unlocks another level of connection to your inner child.

And finally, remember that no matter how old we are, it's important to forgive ourselves and others for past mistakes; don't get too caught up in trying to make things perfect—perfection often comes at the expense of spontaneity which is key here! Instead, you can focus on having fun. Rediscovering your sense of wonder doesn't mean everything has to be perfect—just let go for once and see what happens!

Practicing Self-Expression and Self-Awareness

Self-awareness theory is a psychological concept that focuses on the idea of self-reflection and understanding one's own thoughts, feelings, beliefs, behaviors, and attitudes. It recognizes the inner dialogue we have with ourselves and encourages us to be mindful of our reactions to situations. Self-awareness theory states that when people recognize their inner feelings, beliefs, and values, it can help them gain insight into their motivations for action and lead to more adaptive behavior.

Self-awareness is important in many aspects of life because it helps us better understand ourselves and our relationships with others. By taking the time to reflect on how we think, feel, and behave in different situations, we can become more aware of how our actions impact other people. This can help us develop healthier relationships by understanding why others might respond differently than we do in certain scenarios. Additionally, self-awareness helps us identify our strengths and weaknesses so we can work toward becoming better versions of ourselves.

The benefits of self-awareness are many. People who practice self-awareness tend to have improved decision-making skills since they can take a step back from situations before reacting impulsively or emotionally. They also tend to be more resilient to stress since they have a better understanding of how their emotions affect them in certain circumstances. Self-awareness allows us to manage our emotions better so that they do not overpower us when dealing with onerous tasks or situations. Furthermore, being mindful of our behavior helps increase social acceptance and empathy for others. Lastly, self-aware individuals can experience greater peace within themselves as they learn how their internal dialogues influence their everyday lives.

Self-expression is the act of expressing oneself or one's feelings, thoughts, ideas, opinions, and beliefs in a creative way. It can involve verbal communication such as writing and speaking, nonverbal communication such as art forms like drawing and painting, and physical activities like dance. Self-expression allows us to explore our experiences, emotions, and passions without judgment or criticism.

Self-expression is vitally important because it brings forth our individual freedom. This serves as a source of strength that we can tap into when faced with overwhelming external pressures while simultaneously providing us with insight into our deepest desires so that we may make conscious decisions based on what truly matters most in life. In addition, it helps us form meaningful connections with others by allowing them into our private world that would not otherwise exist if we were just presenting a facade instead of living authentically.

Self-expression can help reduce stress, improve communication with others, provide an outlet for negative emotions like anger or sadness, and boost creativity. Self-expression can also foster greater self-awareness and understanding of one's own needs and values, and cultivate positive relationships with others by being open to authentic connection and dialogue while embracing differences in opinion. Besides this, it can also help increase resilience, which enables people to become more adaptive and find solutions to challenging situations more easily.

Values associated with self-expression include authenticity, courage, and honesty. By being true to oneself rather than trying to conform to society's expectations or fit into a certain mold, it can lead to greater personal growth and inner peace. Having the courage to express yourself can be especially difficult for those who feel socially isolated or have been silenced in the past. However, it is essential for finding one's unique voice, which has the potential for empowering transformation both internally within one's sense of self and externally when connected with other people through dialogue.

To improve your self-expression skills there are several things you can do:

- Start small by setting aside time each day where you express yourself without judgment—whether this is writing a journal entry about something you experienced that day or making art based on your feelings.

- Reflect upon what ideas, feelings or experience matter most deeply to you so that you know how best to truly express yourself from a place of authenticity.

- Be vulnerable with yourself, as facing your fears is part of the path toward becoming comfortable expressing yourself openly.

- Practice communicating openly about how you feel in safe environments such as group therapy sessions or talking circles.

- Connect with your body through movement with activities like dancing. This is another excellent way to express yourself since physical movements often contain deep emotional truths.

- Allow mistakes and accept imperfections. Redirecting your attention will free up energy so that instead of worrying about getting everything "right" you can concentrate on being present in moments that bring joy.

Ultimately engaging in a regular practice of self-expression will provide valuable insights into who we are at our core while giving us permission to honor ourselves exactly as we are—faults and all—without needing approval from anyone else. As long as we remain curious about our inner truth while having compassion toward ourselves, any progress made will lead us closer to understanding our full potential. Then we can live an empowered life filled with meaning and purpose.

Practicing self-expression to heal your inner child is essential in order to become in tune with your emotional and physical well-being. It is important to have a deep understanding of who we are, our values and beliefs, and what expression feels right for us. We should share our true selves with others and not be afraid of expressing who we are. To truly express ourselves we must display resilience, positivity, bravery, and most importantly self-love.

Resilience can be built by accepting our flaws as part of us. By recognizing that mistakes are a part of life, it helps us to develop the strength needed to move forward from difficult situations without feeling overwhelmed or defeated. When faced with challenging times, remind yourself of your capabilities and remember to stay strong for yourself.

Positivity can be cultivated by celebrating small wins no matter how big or small they may be. Releasing positive energy into the world, such as gratitude for all that we have been blessed with allows us to stay focused on the good things instead of wallowing in our misfortune. In times like these, it is more important than ever before to remain hopeful and optimistic despite difficulty or hardship.

Bravery allows us the opportunity to take risks when necessary. This could be anything from having an honest conversation with somebody you trust or simply speaking up when something doesn't feel right even if you fear being judged or ridiculed by others. Taking risks leads to growth, so it's important to find the courage within ourselves even when faced with uncertainty or danger.

Lastly, self-love is essential in order for one's inner child's healing journey to continue unhindered—it provides a sense of security which gives us strength during hard times and encourages us not to give up on ourselves when faced with adversity. Taking time out for yourself every day is key in order to cultivate feelings of love toward oneself; this could involve taking a bubble bath, reading a book, or exercising—whatever relaxes you ultimately sets the tone for how much love you show yourself each day.

PART 2:

REPROGRAMMING
YOUR LIFE

4

NURTURING STRATEGIES AND RADICAL SELF-LOVE

econnecting with your inner child and learning how to play again is a crucial part of inner child work. But it's not the only thing that needs to be done. Another important element of inner child work is learning how to nurture yourself. In this chapter, we'll look at simple and effective strategies for nurturing your inner child, such as releasing anger and pain from caregivers to practicing proper self-care.

We'll look at how nurturing yourself leads to radical transformation in your life, from increased self-love to improved relationships. You'll learn how to create a supportive environment and habits that will help you work through the pain from your inner child's wounds. Finally, this chapter will guide you on your journey to a deep understanding of self-love, so you heal from the past and be in tune with your true feelings.

RELEASING THE BLAME AND ANGER YOU FEEL TOWARD YOUR CAREGIVER(S)

Our inner child acts out because of pain, resentment, anger, and many other emotions. Most times, we may hold anger or resentment against our caregivers for the traumas they bestowed upon us. Holding onto anger toward our parents or caregivers can hurt us and our inner child. These negative emotions can spiral and lead to an array of other negative feelings, such as sadness, depression, anxiety, and even physical ailments. It can also painfully pierce our self-esteem, which can leave us feeling unworthy and unlovable. We may experience difficulty forming meaningful connections with others if we have unresolved issues with our parents or caregivers.

In order to forgive and heal from the anger, it is important to first acknowledge the anger that is present. This recognition allows us to face what has happened, understand why we feel the way we do about our parents or caregivers, and begin the process of healing. We should then talk openly about what has happened with someone we trust who will validate our feelings without judgment. During this process, it is important for us to remember that we did not cause all the pain and trauma in the relationship, recognizing that both parties handle what occurred.

Forgiveness begins with giving ourselves permission to be angry, yet still loving ourselves despite these feelings. Self-forgiveness helps to create space for healing. We may find it helpful to write down our thoughts or engage in other creative practices, like art or music, as a form of release. Establishing boundaries with our parents or caregivers can help protect us from further pain while allowing us to keep them in our lives in whatever capacity works best for us.

It may be beneficial to consider their story as well—understanding their perspective may offer insight into why they behaved the way they did toward us growing up. Although bringing closure through conversation is a powerful tool, it is not always possible, so acceptance is key. When we can't have closure or change a situation accordingly, we can practice accepting that things will not change but that we have the power within ourselves to move on from this pain. Finally, giving yourself love and compassion is essential; treating ourselves with kindness helps cultivate inner peace and acceptance, which allows for true healing of old wounds and nurturing of your inner child.

BUILD A NEW CAREGIVER AND BE YOUR OWN PARENT

Self-parenting is becoming your own parent or primary caregiver. It involves nurturing yourself in the same way that an understanding, supportive parent would nurture their child. It also includes taking responsibility for your own emotional needs in order to heal from past trauma. This form of self-care can help to develop greater emotional resilience, self-compassion, and self-awareness.

When we are young, our caregivers shape how we view ourselves and the world around us. Unfortunately, not all children have been fortunate enough to experience supportive caregiving environments. If you were raised in an environment that was lacking in love and understanding, it's difficult to feel safe within yourself as an adult. Self-parenting can be viewed as a form of reparenting, as it helps adults to reconnect with the neglected parts of themselves and provides them with the security they never had as children.

When practicing self-parenting, adults must become aware of their inner dialogue and actively respond to it in compassionate ways. Instead of being cruel or dismissive toward yourself when something goes wrong, you need to be kind and encouraging. In a traditional parenting role, this is achieved by validating a child's feelings (even if you don't agree with them). Validating their feelings will help them feel heard and understood—this is equally important for adults who are healing through self-parenting, too.

It's also important for adults engaging in self-parenting to practice radical acceptance. This means accepting all aspects of yourself without judgment or criticism—including emotions, behaviors, or beliefs which may have been conditioned into you during childhood that no longer serve you well today. It's about allowing yourself the freedom to be who you really are without feeling ashamed or inadequate for any aspect of yourself—because ultimately nobody is perfect!

Finally, taking part in regular activities which promote relaxation, such as yoga or meditation, can help support your mental well-being while engaging in self-parenting work. These techniques can help you stay grounded throughout the journey back home to your true, authentic self.

Understanding Conscious Self-Parenting

Conscious parenting is a mindful approach to raising children and prioritizing their well-being. It is about understanding the importance of providing a healthy environment for raising children while being aware of the impact that one's own behavior can have on a child's development. By attending to both the child's needs and our own, we create an atmosphere of connection and safety, establishing a strong bond between parent and child.

When it comes to self-parenting or reparenting, conscious parenting can be incredibly helpful. This type of parenting encourages us to become more aware of how our own experiences as children might inform our behavior and approach when it comes to parenting. We can work on healing unresolved issues from our childhoods and strive to mitigate any unhealthy patterns in ourselves that we may have unintentionally passed down to our children.

Practicing radical self-love is also essential to conscious parenting. Self-care activities such as meditation, yoga, journaling, and even just spending time alone can all help us nurture ourselves and build up our physical, mental, and emotional resilience. When we take care of ourselves first, we can be much better equipped for taking care of others around us—including our children.

Validation from parents serves as an important part of conscious parenting too—it allows children to feel seen in their emotions and experiences without judgment or criticism from adults. Reparenting yourself includes allowing oneself space for validating those parts within us that may never have been validated in childhood. Instead of shame or guilt, we can heal through compassion by acknowledging where we've been hurt or wronged, as well as embracing ourselves completely as individuals along the way.

By practicing conscious parenting methods such as self-parenting/reparenting, self-care activities, and validating one's inner child, we give ourselves space for growth in order to be the best caregivers possible for our inner child. This sets you up with some tools you will need throughout life while also learning how to practice self-love along the way.

The Integrated Adult

The integrated adult is an idea within psychodynamic psychology that refers to the development of a healthy, autonomous sense of self by integrating and reconciling all aspects of one's identity. This includes both conscious and unconscious aspects, such as the ego, superego, and id.

The ego is the part of the self that is conscious and rational, while the superego is the part of the self that incorporates idealistic values and morals. The id, on the other hand, is composed of primitive instincts that can be constructive or destructive. Thus, when all these aspects of one's identity are integrated into a cohesive whole, a person can become more authentic and develop a greater sense of self.

Introjections are internalized attitudes or beliefs about ourselves or others that were gained during childhood or even adulthood. They typically originate from our upbringing and formative relationships with others in our environment. For example, if we were raised by parents who had expectations of perfectionism, we may come to believe that anything less than perfect is unacceptable. These beliefs can lead to feelings of shame and self-criticism when we cannot meet those high standards set forth by our parents or caregivers.

The integrated adult can help heal the inner child by providing positive role models for healthy growth and development. Through carefully examining our own beliefs and patterns of behavior, we can find new ways to accept ourselves as we are while also working toward creating a better version of ourselves. As adults, it's important to create a safe space for ourselves where mistakes are accepted instead of judged harshly; this attitude allows us to learn from those mistakes instead of simply condemning them.

Additionally, it's useful for adults to practice self-compassion so that they can forgive themselves for any missteps taken along the way as they seek inner healing and growth. The integrated adult can also provide guidance on how to effectively manage emotions like anger or fear in order to control feelings that might be limiting our potential as individuals. By understanding how emotions affect us cognitively as well as physically and taking steps toward healthier emotional regulation strategies—like finding hobbies that help us relax—we can bond and heal our inner child.

The Four Pillars of Reparenting

The four pillars of reparenting are central tenets to embracing a radical self-love lifestyle. According to Stacey (2021), the four pillars are discipline, joy, emotional regulations, and self-care. By practicing these four elements of reparenting one can create balance in their life while taking steps toward self-care and nurturing their inner child.

Discipline can be seen as a tool used to set limits and boundaries for ourselves intending to improve our lives overall. It allows us to recognize what behaviors are acceptable or prohibited within our own lives, allowing us to prioritize our well-being above all else. When implemented in a comprehensive way with consistency and kindness, discipline can help foster positive habits over time, which will lead to long-term success.

Joy is related to finding purpose through meaningful activities that increase happiness and satisfaction. This could include developing routines or rituals that encourage positive emotions such as gratitude or optimism and making time for hobbies or interests. Joy helps balance work and leisure time while still allowing for personal growth through learning experiences outside of work hours.

Emotional regulation is about understanding where different emotions come from and learning how best to handle them constructively, without judgment or criticism. Then you can express them in healthy ways when needed instead of bottling them up inside yourself. Emotional regulation includes methods such as mindfulness meditation and cognitive reframing techniques. These mindful techniques prompt us to observe our emotions without reacting impulsively or negatively toward ourselves or others involved in the situation at hand.

Finally, self-care involves taking care of oneself from the physical body all the way down into the depths of one's soul. It encompasses everything from proper nutrition and exercise routine with adequate rest all the way up to building strong mental health habits like journaling and daily meditation that give space away from distractions and stressors throughout life's journey. Self-care also entails being kinder and more compassionate toward yourself even when faced with uncomfortable situations, reminding yourself often that you are worth it no matter what life throws at you.

Be the Strict but Loving Parent You Always Wanted

There are various parenting styles that can help with healing the inner child. These styles consist of authoritarian, authoritative, permissive, and uninvolved parenting.

Authoritarian parenting is a style that involves parents setting rules and standards for their children without offering much explanation or flexibility. This style emphasizes obedience and respect for authority figures. Parents who use this style will often have rigid rules that are enforced in a strict manner. This type of parenting is focused on teaching children moral values and desirable behaviors while also expecting them to follow established rules.

Authoritative parenting is like authoritarian parenting in the sense that it focuses on setting clear boundaries and expectations for children. However, unlike with authoritarian parenting, this style allows more room for discussion and negotiation between parents and children. Parents using this approach are more likely to explain why things need to be done a certain way, as well as provide emotional support when necessary. This form of parenting also encourages autonomy by allowing children to make decisions independently within the boundaries set by their parents.

Permissive parenting is a style where the parents allow their children more freedom than what authoritarian or authoritative styles provide. With this type of parenting, there are generally few expectations placed on the child aside from being respectful toward others. While there may be some limits set by the parent, they tend to not be enforced strictly or consistently. Permissive parents often take on a less directive role in their child's life but still provide support when needed.

Uninvolved parenting is one where there is little if any expectations placed upon the child and communication between parent-child is minimal at best. This type of parenting leaves many decisions up to the discretion of the child with very little guidance or monitoring from the parent(s). Oftentimes an uninvolved parent will have limited knowledge about their child's development or activities outside of the home due to a lack of communication about these topics with their child(s).

When trying to determine which type of parenting will help heal your inner child, assess your personal history and beliefs about parental roles. Also, think about how you want your relationship with your inner child(ren) to look like moving forward. Consider how different discipline affects you emotionally as well as how comfortable you feel being more directive vs supporting vs hands-off when interacting with your inner self.

Additionally, it can be helpful to find out which types of parental models were present during childhood. This would help you address any lingering issues from those experiences properly in order for healing to take place effectively and efficiently over time. Ultimately, each person must decide which style works best for them based upon their individual needs. However, understanding what each approach offers can help guide decision-making when it comes time to nurture oneself through reparenting, self-care, and validating one's inner child.

Positive Parenting Tips From Your Parents

Positive parenting techniques can be any strategies that parents use to create an environment of trust, support, understanding, and consistency for their children. Examples of these include setting clear expectations for behavior, providing unconditional love and affection, praising good behavior, and engaging in regular family activities. It's also important to set boundaries and consequences for misbehavior, encourage open communication between parents and child, and model positive behavior. These techniques can all be performed by the self to reconnect and reparent the inner child.

Nurturing healthy relationships is essential in order for us to feel seen, understood, and connected with others—something we all need as human beings. We can do this by learning how to set boundaries around what feels safe for us in terms of certain interactions. by being honest about our wants and needs, and by communicating effectively

Learning how to apologize if we make mistakes or hurt someone's feelings, being kind and respectful toward ourselves and others, and being aware of the power dynamics at play (i.e., not pushing our own agenda onto someone else) are also crucial factors in parenting.

VALIDATING YOUR INNER CHILD

Validating your inner child is the process of providing emotional support, comfort, and understanding to the neglected or abused parts of your inner self. It is a way for adults to reconnect with their past selves and make amends for any wrongs that may have been done in childhood. This process encourages adults to be their own best friend and heal themselves from the inside out.

Validating your inner child means acknowledging and accepting all the emotions, thoughts, and experiences that have occurred throughout your entire life. It includes recognizing both positive and negative emotions as valid parts of yourself and giving them space to express themselves freely without judgment or criticism. The goal is to nurture a safe place within yourself where you can accept your emotional needs without fear of being judged or rejected by others.

Validating your inner child is an important step in healing trauma from our pasts that may still affect us today. Allowing ourselves to feel our emotions openly instead of pushing them away creates a healthier relationship with ourselves, which leads to healthier relationships with others. It also teaches us how to take better care of our mental well-being. We can choose to engage in self-care activities rather than engaging in unhealthy coping mechanisms such as substance abuse or destructive behavior.

How To Validate Your Inner Child

1. Acknowledge your feelings: Start by taking some time alone each day to recognize all the feelings you are experiencing, both positive and negative. Allow yourself to really sit with each emotion without judgment so that you can fully understand it before attempting to move on from it.

2. Create boundaries for yourself: Setting boundaries for yourself will help protect you from external influences while allowing yourself space to explore what it means to be true to who you are without fear of judgment or criticism from others. Note situations that make you feel uncomfortable or unsupported and make sure that those boundaries are respected by other people around you as well.

3. Speak kindly to yourself: Talking kindly about yourself is one way to make sure that your inner child knows they are heard, loved, accepted, and supported no matter what happens in life. Be mindful of the words we use, but also of our body language when speaking about ourselves— sit up straight, smile often, and give compliments whenever possible!

4. Find healthy ways to express emotions: Set aside time each day for self-expression activities such as writing down your thoughts in a journal, drawing, or painting something that expresses how you're feeling inside. Additionally, engaging in physical activity such as yoga or walking can provide an outlet for stress relief while allowing you to connect more deeply with yourself on an emotional level.

5. Spend time with people who support you: We all need people around us who genuinely love and support us unconditionally. These people can remind us how special we truly are despite any challenges we may face along the way! Whether this means spending more quality time with family members or finding new friends who share similar values as yours, surround yourself with those who bring out the best version of yourself. This will help you keep growing into a stronger version of yourself every day.

Phrases and Sayings Your Inner Child Needs to Hear

Aside from validating your inner child, there are other ways to nurture them and bring out the best in you. One way is by telling yourself powerful phrases that your inner child needs to hear. These phrases will help you build trust and understanding with your inner child in order to create lasting change. Some phrases to consider telling your inner child are:

- I love you: When our inner child is feeling neglected, unloved, and unworthy, this simple phrase can be incredibly powerful. Let your inner child know they are loved unconditionally and always, no matter what thoughts or emotions they are experiencing.

- I hear you: Oftentimes, our inner child feels unheard and overlooked. Acknowledge their feelings—whether it be sadness, anger, fear or joy—and let them know you hear them and understand their point of view.

- I'm sorry: Taking responsibility for our own actions and behaviors is important when healing our inner child. Apologizing sincerely to your inner child will allow them to feel heard and validated in their feelings.

- You didn't deserve what happened: Our inner child may often feel like the things that happened to them were deserved or somehow their fault. It's important to remind them that the negative things that have happened in the past do not define who they are now or who they will become in the future.

- Thank you: Expressing gratitude to your inner child helps foster a sense of self-love, showing appreciation for all the hard work they do every day to take care of themselves.

- I forgive you: When we don't forgive ourselves for mistakes we've made in the past it can have a detrimental effect on our well-being both now and in the future. Letting your inner child know you forgive them can help them release any guilt or shame associated with those errors in judgment and allow them to move forward with a fresh slate.

- You did your best: Oftentimes children don't feel successful if they haven't achieved something perfect or done better than others around them; however, simply doing your best should always be rewarded with praise and encouragement, no matter how small the accomplishment may seem at first glance. Remind your inner child that you are proud of their efforts now even if success didn't come right away—because eventually, it will come when they least expect it.

REMEMBER—SELF-CARE IS SELF-PARENTING

Self-parenting and healing the inner child is an important aspect of self-care and personal growth. It involves developing the skills necessary to become the parent you want to be, fostering self-awareness and understanding your feelings as well as providing yourself with discipline and joy.

The first step to self-parenting is knowing what kind of parent you want to be. This can include developing qualities such as patience, kindness, compassion, understanding, and respect. Setting boundaries for yourself is also important when it comes to self-parenting so that you can ensure that you are taking care of yourself in a healthy way.

Developing the skills needed to self-parent is essential in order to provide yourself with a safe environment where you can learn and grow. Learning how to set healthy boundaries for yourself, communicate effectively, and manage your emotions are all beneficial skills that will help you in your journey of self-parenting.

Fostering self-awareness is also an important part of self-parenting as it allows us to explore our emotional landscape so that we can gain insight into our feelings and needs. Taking the time for regular mindfulness practice can be beneficial as it helps us become more aware of our thoughts, emotions, and bodily sensations.

Practicing self-care is another key element when it comes to healing the inner child. Self-care provides us with a safe space where we can take time out from life's demands to relax and recharge our batteries. Setting aside time each day or week dedicated solely to ourselves and doing activities such as reading a book, going for a walk, or having a bath are all good ways of practicing self-care.

Acknowledging and honoring our feelings is another important part of healing the inner child; allowing ourselves to feel our emotions without judgment or criticism can help us better understand ourselves on an emotional level. Journaling can also be beneficial here, giving us an outlet for expressing any difficult thoughts or feelings we are struggling with at any given moment in time.

Learning discipline is also beneficial when it comes to making sure that we prioritize our own well-being over other commitments in life. Learning techniques such as using timers or setting daily reminders on your phone can help you stay focused on tasks throughout the day whilst ensuring that your own needs are met too.

Finally, finding joy and purpose in everyday activities helps ensure that we have positive experiences throughout our day which encourages growth within ourselves rather than feeling overwhelmed by life's demands. Simple pleasures such as watching sunsets, drinking tea, or walking barefoot on grass can bring moments of joy which ultimately nourish both body and soul offering much-needed comfort during times of stress or anxiety.

CHAPTER

5

PRIORITIZING HEALTHY RELATIONSHIPS WITH SELF AND OTHERS

As people grow older, they tend to focus more on external relationships and forget to build healthy relationships with their own selves. Or if your inner child is really wounded, you might lack relationships with others as well. However, your relationships with yourself and others play an important role in making you a well-rounded individual. Healthy relationships can help you become more open and self-aware, allowing you to access inner peace and happiness. In this chapter, we will explore why relationships are important and how to prioritize healthy relationships with yourself and others.

YOUR INNER CHILD AND YOUR RELATIONSHIPS: WHAT'S THE CORRELATION?

Your inner child is an important part of your subconscious that can have a significant effect on how you interact with others. When this part of you is not acknowledged and nurtured, it can lead to problematic behaviors or feelings in relationships. If your inner child is not in check, it may cause you to recreate the same scenarios repeatedly as a way of seeking out the love and validation that it didn't get as a child. This can lead to issues such as difficulty in expressing your needs clearly, difficulty trusting others, difficulty setting boundaries, or an inability to feel secure in relationships.

Signs That Your Inner Child is Affecting Your Relationships

If your inner child has been wounded, it can prevent you from developing healthy relationships. Here are some signs that your inner child is affecting your relationships:

- Difficulty expressing your needs: If your inner child isn't being heard and validated, you may struggle to express yourself effectively during conflicts in relationships. You may remain silent when something bothers you or cannot articulate what exactly is wrong without sounding overly emotional or too reactionary.

- Difficulty trusting others: It's hard to trust anyone if your inner child doesn't feel safe because of past experiences or trauma. As a result, you may be overly cautious when getting into new relationships or even start pushing away those close to you due to fear of being hurt again.

- Difficulty setting boundaries: Because of their need for approval, an unchecked inner child can make it difficult for someone to draw healthy boundaries with others when needed. They may find themselves trying so hard to please everyone else that they forget about their own wants and needs, causing them resentment later on.

- Inability to feel secure in relationships: An unchecked inner child can also lead one to feel constantly insecure in their current relationship. This can lead them down a path of constant comparison and questioning if they are good enough for their partner. This kind of behavior only leads to further feelings of insecurity, which then creates a vicious cycle where they never truly feel secure in the relationship no matter how well things go initially.

- Staying in toxic, abusive, or incompatible relationships: Without a nurtured inner child, some people may find themselves staying in relationships that are not meant for them. This could be a result of an inability to express wants and needs or feeling like they don't deserve better.

- You fear being vulnerable, intimacy, and connection: Not giving attention to your inner child can lead to fear of being vulnerable and opening up in relationships. You may avoid intimacy because you don't feel safe enough to share yourself with another person or lack the trust necessary for connection.

Unhealthy Inner Child Dynamics

If left unchecked, your inner child can manifest itself in forms of unhealthy behavior. You may find yourself engaging in self-sabotaging behaviors like alcohol or drug abuse, refusing to take responsibility for your actions, or avoiding interpersonal connections altogether. Additionally, your inner child can manifest into different archetypes. According to Weber (2015), some of the common wounded inner child archetypes are:

- The tantrum thrower is an unhealthy inner child archetype that is often characterized by a lack of impulse control. They are prone to outbursts of anger and frustration, as well as other issues such as emotional volatility, mood swings, aggression, and extreme reactions to situations. Tantrum throwers often struggle with communication and interpersonal relationships due to their volatile nature. They may find it difficult to express themselves in healthy ways or take responsibility for their actions.

- The master manipulator is another unhealthy inner child archetype that strives to get their own way through any means necessary. They are skilled in the art of persuasion and have an uncanny ability to twist words or situations around until they con people into getting what they want. At its core, manipulation is about controlling those around them for personal gain—be it materialistic or emotional—which can cause harm and disruption in relationships.

- The brave and loyal soldier reflects an unhealthy inner need for approval from others and a fear of abandonment. This archetype will essentially take on any cause or mission that makes them look good in the eyes of those they admire. The Brave and Loyal Soldier seeks validation from external sources instead of looking inward at their true needs or desires; they are also highly susceptible to peer pressure due to their need for acceptance.

- Finally, the rowdy rebel reflects an unhealthy sense of entitlement that fuels reckless behavior and disregard for rules or authority figures. This type of inner child archetype often behaves impulsively without regard for consequences, believing themselves above reproach or punishment.

Rowdy Rebels act out due to feelings of betrayal over past injustices done against them; this defiance may manifest itself into risky behaviors such as substance abuse, delinquency, crime, or self-harm.

If you notice any of these archetypes present in your life, it may be time to nurture your inner child and bring back the joyful wonder of childhood. These archetypes can be signs that your inner child is trying to escape from the pain it has been carrying since childhood and attempting to gain control over something that is out of its control.

FIRST STEP: CULTIVATING A HEALTHY RELATIONSHIP WITH SELF

Developing a healthy relationship with yourself is an essential part of leading a fulfilling life. To do this, you must learn to be kind and accept who you are and practice self-awareness, gratitude, and intentional living.

The first step in cultivating a healthy relationship with oneself is to be grateful and appreciative of your body. Recognizing the beauty of your physical form that allows you to explore the world and experience life can help provide you with feelings of self-worth. Additionally, learning to appreciate the abilities of your body—such as strength, resilience, and adaptability—can help foster a sense of confidence and pride in yourself.

The next step is to let go of perfectionism. It's important not to be too critical or judge yourself harshly when things don't go as planned. Negative criticisms will only tear down your confidence level so surround yourself with positive people who are supportive and encouraging. Understand that it's okay to make mistakes and recognize that attempting perfection will only lead to disappointment and negative self-talk. Instead, focus on progress rather than perfection by setting achievable goals for yourself and celebrating the impact each small step makes toward achieving them.

One way to gain insight into how you feel about yourself is by being intentional in your thoughts and actions. Consistent reflection can help develop greater awareness about one's own thoughts, feelings, beliefs, values, attitudes, habits, behaviors, etc., which will improve overall self-esteem levels over time. Furthermore, being curious about these aspects can lead to greater self-understanding while practicing acceptance will help come to terms with all forms of emotions (both positive and negative).

Finally, developing good habits is another effective way of creating a healthier relationship with oneself. This could include anything from eating healthier foods or exercising regularly to reading books or engaging in creative activities like art or music—whatever suits you best! These habits will not only nourish your mind but also provide structure throughout the day. It will also help cultivate positive thought patterns, which may cause better mental health outcomes in the long run.

Benefits of Having a Healthy Relationship With Self

When you have a healthy relationship with yourself, it can bring many positive benefits to your life. One of the most beneficial things is that you can rely on yourself for both emotional and physical support when times are tough. That sense of self-reliance gives you strength and security which can then be extended to your relationships with others, improving them and making it easier to connect in meaningful ways.

Having a healthy relationship with yourself encourages self-confidence, as you become more comfortable in your own skin and learn to accept yourself for who you are. This allows you to place less emphasis on external validation from other people and move forward with greater confidence in your decisions.

Being able to foster a healthy relationship with yourself can also bring an increased sense of happiness overall. You will become more content and satisfied when engaging in activities that make you happy because of the strong bond that exists between your mind and body. You will also be better equipped to take on any problems or challenges that come your way since the trust and understanding that comes from the relationship help provide clarity while evaluating each situation.

Another significant benefit of having a healthy relationship with yourself is being able to regulate negative emotions more effectively. When faced with difficult situations, rather than letting those emotions run rampant over your actions, being emotionally connected to yourself allows you to be mindful of your mental state without allowing it to control them completely. This results in fewer emotional outbursts due to increased awareness about what's happening internally at any given moment. Lastly, being connected with oneself also allows for a greater presence in all aspects of life which leads to higher concentration levels which ultimately translates into productivity gains across various tasks.

In conclusion, forming a strong connection with oneself has tremendous benefits for every aspect of life, including forming healthy interpersonal relationships, self-confidence levels, and overall mental health. It enables you to develop stronger control over your negative emotions and lead a happier life by becoming more present throughout day-to-day activities. This results in higher effectiveness and improved satisfaction from daily accomplishments.

LETTING GO OF UNHEALTHY RELATIONSHIPS

Letting go of an unhealthy relationship can be a hard process, but it is ultimately necessary for emotional and mental well-being. In order to let go of this type of relationship, one must first determine the problem. Oftentimes, it is difficult to see the bigger picture when you are so close to the issue at hand. It requires stepping back and objectively assessing what has gone wrong with the relationship and why.

Once the issue has been identified, it is important to allow yourself to feel your feelings about it rather than burying them or pushing them away. Talking through these feelings with someone you trust or writing down your thoughts may be a beneficial way to gain perspective on the situation.

After acknowledging and accepting your emotions, reflect on what you have learned from this experience so that similar relationships can be avoided in the future. Ask yourself questions such as, *What did I learn about my boundaries? What did I learn about other people's behaviors? How did this relationship impact me emotionally?* Answering these questions will help you gain insight into how to better protect yourself in the future.

Distance yourself from the person or situation if possible, especially if it involves a romantic partner or family member. This could involve reducing contact with them, limiting time spent together, or even ceasing contact altogether if necessary. Removing reminders of them can also be helpful; delete any pictures they're in from social media, unfollow them online, and remove any physical reminders such as gifts they've given you out of plain sight.

To help you further, it's crucial to remove any filters that may exist such as love goggles. These filters are often present in unhealthy relationships where one partner does not act in their best interest but makes excuses for their behavior by blaming external factors like stress at work or lack of sleep instead of owning up to their part in it all.

Lastly, practice forgiveness and acceptance either for yourself or for those involved in the situation—or both! Forgiveness doesn't mean condoning someone's behavior. Instead, it means allowing yourself to move forward from a place free of anger and resentment toward others involved so that you are no longer stuck living in pain from past events. Acceptance helps us recognize that although we may want things to turn out differently than they did, we must accept reality for what it is and intentionally choose how we wish to proceed moving forward accordingly.

Drawing Healthy Boundaries

Creating and establishing healthy boundaries is essential for upholding personal values, beliefs, and emotional well-being. Boundaries are limits we set for ourselves, which allow us to be in control of how we interact with the world around us. This includes setting limits on how much time we spend with friends or family members, the amount of emotional support we can provide to others at any given time, and even the type of activities we engage in. Establishing these boundaries can help heal our inner child while also strengthening relationships. Here's how to create and establish healthy boundaries:

1. Reflect on yourself and your needs

To effectively create healthy boundaries, it is important to take some time to reflect on what you truly need out of a situation or relationship. What are your values and beliefs? Asking yourself questions like these will help you identify what you need in order to remain emotionally safe and secure.

2. Make small adjustments

Rather than making drastic changes in one fell swoop, start by making small adjustments first. This can include setting aside more "me" time into your schedule, limiting contact with certain individuals or groups that make you uncomfortable, or saying no to things that don't align with your values or goals, etc. Making incremental progress toward creating healthier boundaries will keep you from feeling overwhelmed or discouraged as you begin this process

3. Implement your boundaries early on

In order for these boundaries to be effective and respected by others, it is vital to implement them as early as possible within a relationship or situation—before any feelings get hurt or misunderstandings arise. Making sure everyone involved understands what you expect from the onset will ensure that everyone feels seen and heard from the start.

4. Be consistent

Once established, it's vital to remain consistent when enforcing healthy boundaries within a relationship or situation. This is especially crucial if those around you aren't used to this behavior from you yet. Remaining firm but fair when interacting with others can help create an environment where respect for personal boundaries is valued and appreciated by all parties involved over time.

5. Establish framework

Setting up a framework for how things should proceed (i.e., how often communication should take place between two people) helps create an expectation that can be followed consistently while also allowing room for flexibility if needed later down the line.

6. Gain perspective

It's helpful to gain perspective during this process by talking with friends or family members who may have experienced similar situations themselves (or perhaps even engaging in counseling!). Asking questions such as "How did they navigate this specific challenge?" can help provide helpful direction on ways of successfully implementing effective boundary-setting strategies in various situations.

7. Be your own cheerleader

While creating healthy boundaries isn't always easy at first, it's important not to forget about self-care during this process. Giving yourself positive affirmations throughout may help bolster motivation when times get tough; reminding yourself why creating healthier boundaries is so important in order for relationships (with both yourself and other individuals).

Cultivating Healthy Relationships

Cultivating healthy relationships is an important part of life. Developing a strong, nurturing, and honest connection with another person can be incredibly rewarding and enriching. In order to ensure that your relationships are as positive and healthy as possible, there are several key steps you can take to foster growth.

The first step in cultivating healthy relationships is, to be honest, and authentic. It's important to be sincere in your communication with others, and avoid making excuses or fabricating stories. Be true to yourself and open about your feelings, thoughts, and ideas. It's also important to recognize the other person for who they are, without judgment or prejudice. Everyone has their own unique story and perspective that should be respected and appreciated.

Communication is also key when it comes to cultivating healthy relationships; it allows you to express yourself clearly while showing empathy toward the other person. Listening actively is just as important as expressing yourself; taking time to really understand what the other person is saying can help create a better connection between the two of you. It's also essential to compromise during disagreements—neither party should always get their way all the time without considering the other's perspective on the matter at hand.

In order for a relationship to remain healthy, it must also be reliable and fair. Trust must be earned by both parties in order for a relationship to thrive; if this trust breaks down, then so does the relationship itself. In addition, each person within the relationship should have an equal footing regarding decisions made and any conflicts that may arise along the way. Both parties should have their voices heard equally during discussions or debates.

Overall, nurturing healthy relationships requires effort from everyone involved—but when done right it can create lifelong memories with friends, family, or partners that will last forever! By being honest and authentic, communicating openly with empathy, and being reliable and fair—you can build positive connections that foster mutual growth amongst those around you!

CHAPTER

6

LIVING UNPRETENTIOUSLY: BE YOURSELF AND PROUDLY SO

We often try to put on a mask and pretend to be someone else, but living unpretentiously is the best way to be true to ourselves. This means being proud of who you are and unapologetically expressing your true self. In this chapter, we will explore how to break free from the idea of perfection and live authentically. We will look at the reasons we often feel compelled to wear a mask, discuss the power of vulnerability, and offer tips for living unpretentiously.

We will discuss how to be honest with yourself and those around you, avoid getting caught up in comparison and judgment, and accept yourself as you are. Living authentically is not a straightforward process, but the rewards can be profound. Not only will it help you build healthier relationships, but it will bring a newfound sense of peace and joy.

WHAT BEING AUTHENTIC MEANS

Being authentic means being true to oneself, being honest with oneself and others, and genuinely expressing one's thoughts, feelings, and beliefs. It is about understanding and accepting who we are in our entirety—our strengths, weaknesses, gifts, talents, flaws, and quirks. When we are authentic, we recognize the power of our unique perspectives and share them without fear or judgment. Authenticity allows us to be vulnerable yet strong enough to embrace all that makes us who we are.

Authenticity is important for both our well-being and for healing our inner child because it allows us to fully express ourselves without fear of criticism or judgment from others. Being authentic gives us permission to honor our unique selves. We are giving a voice to the parts of us that have been hidden away due to uncomfortable experiences in the past or external pressures to conform. Without authenticity, it is impossible to grow as individuals. An essential part of growth is truthfulness—being honest with ourselves about who we really are and what we truly need.

When we live authentically, it enables us to have meaningful relationships with ourselves first. Then we can engage in other capacities, like romantic partnerships, friendships, family relationships, etc. These interactions can be based on a foundation of trust built on self-awareness rather than false pretenses or masks used as a protection mechanism against hurtful memories from the past. Besides this trust between self and other(s), living authentically also helps foster a deep sense of self-acceptance which is vital for forming healthy relationships with people around us; if we cannot accept who we are then how can we expect others to?

The benefits of being authentic include being able to experience life more deeply through genuine exploration rather than relying on surface-level connections or expectations set by societal standards. It also allows us to create meaningful connections across different areas such as work, career, ambition, and personal or family life since there isn't a disconnect between how you show up at work versus home, etc. Last but not least, being authentic builds resilience by strengthening your sense of self-worth. Even during challenging times, you can still access that core belief that you are worthy despite any external criticism or rejection you may face.

WHY BEING YOUR AUTHENTIC SELF MIGHT BE DIFFICULT AT TIMES

Being your authentic self might be difficult at times because of the way our brains are wired. We have developed to prioritize safety and security, so it is natural for us to shy away from anything that we perceive as too risky or different. This can make it hard to express our true selves when we fear others may not approve of or accept us. It is also important to remember that being your authentic self doesn't always mean going against the grain; it just means being honest with yourself about who you are and what you want.

In order to be true to ourselves, we often have to slow down and really think about what we want out of life. This process requires introspection, which can feel like a daunting task if we don't take the time to do it. We tend to rush through life, creating routines and habits that keep us on autopilot and distraction-free. Taking the time to get off of this path and check in with ourselves can be intimidating but is a necessary part of living authentically.

Finally, many people struggle with being their true selves because they feel like it would make them seem selfish or inconsiderate of the wants and needs of others. However, making sure you are taking care of yourself first before tending to those around you does not always mean forsaking other people's feelings; it simply means knowing your own boundaries and values well enough that you can make decisions based on them rather than worry about how others will view them.

Overall, being your authentic self is something that takes practice and patience in order for us all to fully understand our core values and desires. It can seem overwhelming at times due to society's expectations, our evolutionary need for safety, or feeling obligated toward others. However, if we take the time to build a better understanding of what makes us unique individuals, then this process becomes much easier. It allows us space for growth while ensuring we remain true to our innermost truths throughout life's ups and downs.

THERE'S NO AUTHENTICITY WITHOUT SELF-ACCEPTANCE

There's no authenticity without self-acceptance. Many people struggle with self-acceptance, but they often confuse it with self-esteem. The two are very different, yet both are necessary to cultivate a sense of authenticity in our lives. Self-esteem is the appraisal of one's own worth or value. It is based on how one perceives themselves and how they measure up against society's standards. On the other hand, self-acceptance is accepting oneself for who we are regardless of society's standards or accomplishments. This is where true authenticity can be found because it requires us to accept all parts of ourselves—both the good and bad—in order to be genuine and honest with ourselves and with others.

When we practice self-acceptance, we open ourselves up to an overall sense of well-being and contentment. We become more secure in who we are as individuals, understanding that we don't need to change anything about ourselves just to please others or fit in with societal norms. We also learn how to better express our authentic selves without fear or judgment.

This allows us to build meaningful relationships with others that are based on mutual acceptance rather than attachment or control. Additionally, when we practice self-acceptance, it gives us the freedom to explore new activities and interests without feeling hindered by a lack of self-confidence or approval from outside sources. We can trust our own instincts and decisions without worrying that others will disagree or criticize us for them.

Being authentic also helps us develop better problem-solving skills since there is no internal struggle between what you truly believe versus what you feel would please those around you most. In other words, practicing self-acceptance will help us answer the troublesome questions faster since our judgment won't be clouded by bias from outside sources who may not have our best interest at heart.

Moreover, authenticity leads to healthier emotional regulation which makes it easier for us to process stressors in our daily lives instead of bottling them up inside until it becomes overwhelming. However, this can all be avoided by embracing our true selves during times of distress instead of turning away from who we really are out of fear of not being accepted by others.

Overall, there is no authenticity without true self-acceptance. The quality encourages us to be vulnerable and honest enough with ourselves so that we can take off the masks that keep us from connecting authentically with ourselves and those around us. Only then can we learn how crucial inner peace is for leading a happy life full of fulfillment and joy regardless of where we stand compared to society's standards.

10 POWERFUL STRATEGIES FOR BEING YOUR AUTHENTIC SELF

Authenticity is critical to developing healthy relationships—not only with yourself but also with others. Here are ten strategies for reclaiming your true self and building healthier relationships:

1. Taking a personal and moral inventory

Taking the time to examine your values, beliefs, and motivations is essential to understanding who you are and how you express yourself authentically. This inventory can be an ongoing process that helps you understand where your morals come from, what motivates your decisions, and how they affect your behavior. Through this examination of yourself, it can help to gain clarity on what you believe, and feel is right or wrong which helps with being authentic in the choices that you make. It also helps to identify issues that may cause inner conflicts or keep you from being true to yourself.

2. Building a social support system

Having a strong support system allows us to feel more secure in expressing ourselves authentically as we know people are there for us no matter what we do or don't do. This support system could comprise family members, friends, colleagues or mentors who will listen without judgment when we need someone to talk to about our struggles with authenticity. With a network of people who understand our challenges and want the best for us, we can gain the strength we need to stay true even when things get tough.

3. Being truthful and assertive

Being truthful means speaking openly and honestly about who we are and what matters most to us as individuals—regardless if others agree or not. We also have the right to respectfully assert our opinions while still respecting those of others; this allows us to hold our ground while still maintaining respect for other people's beliefs which is important when remaining authentic in our interactions with them. Speaking up with confidence when necessary will also help build trust between ourselves and others which ultimately leads to greater authenticity with each other over time.

4. Recognizing internal versus external influences

Knowing the difference between internal influences (your own desires) versus external influences (others' wishes) is essential for determining if something is truly authentic for you or if it's just something that everyone else expects from you. Doing so allows for greater self-awareness on whether or not a decision aligns with your values; it also enables us to better articulate why something is important for us should anyone question our actions or decisions down the line.

5. Developing prism thinking

This involves looking at an issue from all angles before making a decision. It's crucial to weigh both sides carefully until you find a solution that works best for you as an individual rather than trying to fit into any preconceived notions society may have imposed upon you as "the right thing" to do, say, or think, etc. By doing so, it allows one to maintain autonomy over their own choices while still understanding varying perspectives that exist outside of their personal bubble. This allows one to make decisions that reflect their true self instead of succumbing to peer pressure. Peer pressure often leads toward leading an inauthentic life instead where one simply follows societal norms instead of feeling free enough to express one's unique self while still considering alternative viewpoints on certain matters.

6. Find the good in each situation:

We often focus on the negative things that come our way and overlook the positive. Instead of letting the negativity of what went wrong consume us, why not choose to find the positives in every situation? Whether it's finding a silver lining in an argument or reframing a tough moment into something with potential for growth and learning, actively seeking the good can help you stay authentic and feel more empowered.

7. Understand that there is only one of you

It's easy to get lost in comparison with others—their looks, their accomplishments, their lifestyle—and forget that there's only one you. Embrace who you are and what makes you unique; no one else has had your same experiences or perspectives, which means your life path will never be exactly like anyone else's. Accept yourself for who you are right now, flaws and all, and don't fit into someone else's box if it doesn't fit your goals or values.

8. Take inspired action daily:

Don't just go through life costing from day to day; become inspired by taking proactive steps toward achieving your goals—even if they feel small or insignificant. This kind of motivated behavior will help you stay focused on being true to yourself and living out your dreams without worrying about what other people think.

9. Practice being honest and dealing with uncomfortable situations

Many people shy away from being honest because of fear. They fear hurting someone's feelings or fear negative consequences. However, it's important to remember that being honest is an act of self-love rather than selfishness. Learning how to express yourself honestly while still being respectful can be daunting but necessary practice in staying true to yourself in any environment. The same goes for uncomfortable situations; although they may be difficult at first, practice expressing yourself authentically as much as possible so that eventually it becomes second nature when facing challenging conversations or scenarios

10. Create a life you're proud of

Living authentically should never mean settling for less than what makes you happy; dream big and create a life that fills your heart with pride! Start by writing down your goals and aspirations; take some time each day (even if it's just five minutes) to visualize what that life looks like for you. What do your job, home, and relationships look like? Then use this visual reminder as motivation to keep pursuing the most authentic version of yourself possible!

With these 10 authentic living tips, you can begin building healthy relationships with yourself and others, which are essential to your well-being. Remember that being authentic means accepting all of yourself, including the flaws, and validating even of your own mistakes. Taking the time to nurture yourself is a necessary part of healing any wounds that are preventing you from living your best life.

PRACTICING AUTHENTICITY WORKSHEETS

There are three parts to this authenticity worksheet. To be authentic, you must first show up to the present. Then you must know and understand your truth so that you can express it. Finally, you must act on your truth in order to be seen and heard. Below are prompts to help guide you through the authenticity worksheet.

Part One: Show Up

The first step is to show up and be present. Becoming aware of your inner child requires you to make time for yourself, be honest with yourself, and reflect on your experiences. To do this, you need to be aware, acknowledge, and accept all aspects of yourself—the good, the bad, and the ugly.

Awareness

Take a moment to assess where you are right now. How do you feel? What is your body telling you? Are you tense, relaxed, or somewhere in between? What thoughts are running through your mind? Are they positive, negative, or neutral? What do I need at this moment?

....

....

....

....

....

....

Acknowledging

Take ownership of your feelings, thoughts, and experiences. It's important to acknowledge that these are part of you and accept them as they are. Can you name how you're feeling? What emotions are present?

....

....

....

....

....

....

Acceptance

Once you have become aware and acknowledged how you're feeling within, it's time to accept them. Acceptance doesn't mean that you agree with the way things are, but rather that you acknowledge it as part of your journey and take responsibility for it. Take six slow deep breaths and sit with the thoughts or feelings you're experiencing. Don't engage in them, just observe them. After the breaths, reflect on how you feel below.

_____

_____

_____

_____

_____

Part Two: Understand Your Truth

The next step is to understand your truth and make sure it aligns with who you really are. To do this, you need to recognize your needs, values, and beliefs. Answer the following fill-in-the-blanks as quickly as possible to determine where fears might hold you back and what beliefs are important to you.

I need _____ to feel secure, accepted, and appreciated.

My values are _____ because they are important to me.

I believe _____ because it helps guide my actions and decisions.

If I wasn't afraid, I would _____ because it's important to me.

I feel safe when _____ because it is a sign of acceptance and appreciation.

I feel fear when _____ because it is a sign of insecurity and lack of self-esteem.

If I do something against my values, I feel _____.

A time I went against my values was _____.

Fear stops me from _____ because I am uncertain and anxious.

Fear shows up in me when _____ because it is a sign of insecurity.

When I am fearful, I _____.

I become uncertain or anxious when _____.

My biggest fears are _____.

What stopped me from accomplishing my goals in the past is _____.

What scares me the most is _____.

If nothing was standing in my way, 10 goals I would accomplish are _____.

Part Three: Act On Your Truth

The last step is to act on your truth and live it out. Now that you have taken the time to become aware, acknowledge, and accept how you feel, it's time to act on them. To do this, you must be able to identify patterns and break free of fear and resistance by making a commitment to yourself and creating a plan.

Identify Patterns

Reflect on the information you have gathered in the previous steps. Examine the patterns and cycles that keep repeating in your life. Is there something you need to let go of? Are there any areas where you need to take action or create boundaries?

Break Free of Fear

Fear is often a sign that we're avoiding change or moving forward. It's helpful to remind yourself that the only way out is through. Remind yourself of your truth and make a commitment to yourself that you will take action in line with it, regardless of how uncomfortable it may be. Take three to five items from the list you created above and make a personal commitment to yourself.

I commit to accomplishing...

Create a Plan

Create an action plan with realistic goals, specific steps to take, and account-ability measures. This will help you stay on track and focus on the things that are most important to you. Use the space below to break your goals into small, actionable steps and brainstorm any ideas of how you can hold yourself accountable.

I will achieve my goal by:

1.

2.

3.

4.

5.

I will hold myself accountable by:

1. ....

2. ....

3. ....

4. ....

5. ....

By following these steps, you will deepen your connection with yourself and honor who you are.

SELF-ACCEPTANCE WORKSHEETS

Self-acceptance can be a difficult process, but it is an important part of inner child work. Self-acceptance worksheets can help you identify areas of your life where you might need to work on accepting yourself more. Follow the prompts below to help identify areas of your life that you could work on becoming more self-accepting.

Understanding Yourself

Where do you want to make a change in your life? Do you want to improve in certain areas, or do you need to let go of something that no longer serves you?

....

....

....

....

....

....

Why do you think this change is necessary? What will it allow you to do that you can't right now? Your "why" is crucial to staying motivated and on track.

If you make this change, what other changes or what shift will you experience? What could you gain or lose if you make this change?

Are you telling yourself any excuses or lies that you should challenge? Are there any beliefs or patterns of behavior that no longer serve you, and if so, what are they?

Are you willing to part ways with these beliefs and take inspired action? What could you do today to start living a more self-accepting life? Once you have identified your areas of growth, it's time to take action and start making the changes that will help you reach true self-acceptance.

How do you feel knowing that you hold the power to make these changes? Does something shift within you internally knowing you have this power? If so, reflect in detail below.

What can you do to keep yourself on track and motivated throughout this journey? How can you remind yourself to live a life of self-love and self-acceptance?

PART 3:

HELPING YOUR INNER CHILD THRIVE

CHAPTER

7

FINDING HEALING THROUGH FORGIVENESS

Forgiveness is one of the most powerful tools for healing our inner child. It helps to release negative energy that prevents us from sharing our authentic selves and having healthy relationships. In this chapter, we will explore the power of forgiveness, which will help you move forward on your journey toward inner peace and happiness.

WHY SELF-FORGIVENESS IS KEY TO HEALING?

Lack of self-forgiveness can manifest in several ways, from feeling guilt and shame to ruminating on mistakes and holding onto grudges. Without forgiving ourselves for our wrongdoings, we can become highly critical of ourselves, feel a lack of self-acceptance, and constantly beat ourselves up over things we've done in the past. We may also struggle with poor self-esteem and depression due to being unable to move past our mistakes and forgive ourselves. This lack of self-forgiveness can be extremely detrimental to our mental health and can prevent us from healing the inner child.

On the other hand, practicing self-forgiveness is key to healing the inner child. Self-forgiveness involves recognizing that while we may have made mistakes in the past, they do not define us or make us unworthy in any way.

This recognition allows us to let go of shame and guilt associated with those mistakes so that we can accept them as part of who we are without dwelling on them or letting them affect our lives negatively.

Self-forgiveness also involves being kinder to ourselves by replacing negative thoughts about ourselves with more positive ones, such as recognizing our strengths instead of focusing on what has been lost or gone wrong in life. Additionally, it means practicing compassion for ourselves when things don't go according to plan; acknowledging that mistakes are inevitable in life, and understanding that it does not mean we are worthless or that we deserve punishment.

For those who are religious, or seek internal validation through mediation, prayer, or spiritual practices, self-forgiveness can involve seeking forgiveness from a higher power. Instead of using our internal voice, we can direct our forgiveness-seeking toward a higher power that we trust and believe in, as this can be a powerful source of comfort and reassurance. However, if you're not religious or believe in a higher power, seeking internal forgiveness may mean engaging in activities that bring joy, love, and peace.

When practiced regularly, self-forgiveness helps us let go of resentment and regret toward ourselves, allowing us to heal our inner child so that they can continue to grow into their full potential free from negative thoughts or emotions associated with past events.

Practicing Forgiveness: How to Let Go of Guilt and Shame

Practicing forgiveness is an important and valuable part of healing the inner child. It requires an understanding of self-acceptance, which is the ability to accept oneself and one's mistakes without judgment or criticism. Self-acceptance is crucial for healing because it allows us to acknowledge our flaws, shortcomings, and limitations without needing to feel ashamed or guilty about them. This helps us to release any self-limiting beliefs and ultimately move forward in a healthier way.

Natural guilt can be difficult to deal with as it requires us to reflect internally on our actions and how they align with our values. In this case, self-forgiveness may help us overcome the mistakes made in the past so that we can rebuild trust in ourselves again. Collective guilt can also be difficult because it involves feeling responsible for something outside of our control which can lead to feelings of helplessness and frustration. Self-forgiveness here could involve understanding that everyone makes mistakes, but that there are still steps we can take as individuals (e.g., advocating for social change) toward resolving this issue in a constructive manner.

Chronic guilt often stems from feeling guilty over things outside of our control such as physical disability or mental illness. However, in this case, forgiveness comes from understanding that everyone is unique and accepting yourself as you are without judgment or criticism. Finally, survivor's guilt often demands recognition and understanding of what was lost. Here practicing forgiveness means coming to terms with the reality that sometimes life does not go according to plan and accepting what happened so that you can start moving on in life rather than dwelling on past experiences.

Self-acceptance is crucial to healing your inner child because forgiveness starts with self-forgiveness. When you stop judging yourself for your mistakes and practice self-compassion, you can start building self-trust which will help you continue on your healing journey without letting negative emotions hold you back. Practicing forgiveness involves allowing yourself to let go of any feelings of shame or regret. Then you can focus on being present in the here and now, loving yourself unconditionally, and being open to learning from mistakes rather than punishing yourself for them. This kind of self-acceptance helps us build healthier relationships with ourselves and others, improve our mental health and create space for growth and healing.

Signs that guilt may be overcoming you are:

- feeling overwhelmed by feelings of guilt and regret

- struggling to move on from past events

- living in the past rather than being present

- constantly judging or criticizing yourself for mistakes made

- feeling disconnected from others because of negative self-talk

If you find yourself struggling with any of these signs, it is important to take the time to practice self-forgiveness and self-acceptance.

Practicing forgiveness is an important part of living a full and meaningful life. To let go of guilt and shame can be challenging, but it is possible with the right approaches and attitude. To start, it's important to explore the source of your guilt or shame—why did it arise in the first place? Are you beating yourself up for something that wasn't actually your fault?

It's also key to take note of the signs associated with feeling guilty or ashamed, such as feeling anxious, unable to concentrate, or having difficulty sleeping. By understanding the feelings you experience because of guilt or shame, you can better address them and start to take steps toward healing.

Once you have identified these signs and explored their source, it is useful to apologize and make amends where appropriate—even if it feels difficult. Apologizing and making amends can help you recognize the impact of your actions and take ownership for them. It may also be beneficial to learn from experiences from the past; understanding what went wrong and how you could do better in future scenarios.

Also, building gratitude into your daily routine can help to combat negative feelings associated with guilt or shame. Gratitude can be as simple as setting aside a few moments every day to acknowledge and cherish what you have and the people around you. This helps to shift perspective and focus on the positive aspects of life rather than dwelling on the negative.

Finally, use guilt as a tool for learning—although it's not always pleasant, ask yourself what this experience might be teaching you about yourself or about others? Can you learn from this in order to be better in the future?

By taking a step back from the situation and reflecting on its significance within a wider context, you may find that there are some positive lessons to be taken away.

PRACTICING SELF-COMPASSION AND ACCEPTANCE

Developing self-compassion and acceptance starts with you taking time to practice self-care and nurture yourself. One way to do this is by practicing self-compassion and affirming self-talk. When we talk to ourselves, it's important that we're making positive statements instead of negative ones. We can encourage ourselves and speak kindly to ourselves, just as we would a good friend. Affirmations can also help us focus on what we want in life rather than dwelling on our perceived shortfalls.

Another powerful tool for developing self-compassion is cultivating gratitude. Practicing gratitude helps us to appreciate what we already have instead of focusing on what's missing from our lives. This practice can be instrumental in helping you develop greater acceptance of yourself and your life.

For developing a deeper understanding and acceptance of who we really are, spending regular time alone, engaging in activities like meditation or journaling can be invaluable. Making an effort to slow down, take some deep breaths, and focus on our thoughts and feelings can help us become more aware of our needs and desires. When we do this, we can better understand our individual triggers so that when challenging situations arise, we know how best to respond or cope with them.

Finally, treating yourself as you would a friend can prompt stronger feelings of self-acceptance. Doing nice things for yourself such as taking breaks during busy days or rewarding yourself with something special after achieving a goal will not only provide immediate benefits but also improve both your mental state and overall emotional well-being over time. So, next time you feel overwhelmed or stressed out, try talking to yourself in the same compassionate way you would speak to someone else; because ultimately being kinder and gentler toward yourself leads not only to greater inner peace but also increased resilience in facing life's challenges head on!

Stop Being a Perfectionist

Being a perfectionist can be highly detrimental to both your mental and physical health. Perfectionists place impossibly high standards on themselves, and when they don't meet them, they experience a deep sense of shame and guilt. These feelings lead to an extreme dissatisfaction with their work, often causing depression and anxiety. Perfectionists also experience physical symptoms such as pains in the chest, stomach problems, and headaches because of the high stress that comes with being a perfectionist.

When you're a perfectionist, there is no room for mistakes or flaws in what you do. You are constantly setting higher goals for yourself and striving for absolute excellence in every task, however small it may be. This often leads to burnout from overworking yourself to reach those unrealistic standards. You may also become increasingly critical of yourself and those around you. This negative attitude can destroy relationships at home, in school, or at work as well as negatively impact your own self-esteem.

People who are perfectionists tend to exhibit certain behaviors. They may work excessively long hours, feel unsatisfied even when all the criteria have been met, set impossible goals, or expect others to meet their standards of "perfection." Additionally, they might procrastinate out of fear of making mistakes, comparing themselves with others, becoming too emotionally invested in their work, and thinking that failure is unacceptable.

There are several strategies that can be used when dealing with perfectionism including challenging negative thoughts, understanding that not everything needs to be perfect, focusing on process instead of outcome, and accepting criticism without being insulted. Also, talking about your difficulties with someone you trust, being kinder to yourself by setting reasonable expectations, and taking breaks often when needed can help manage stress levels caused by trying too hard to achieve "perfection."

Finally, it's important to remember that everyone makes mistakes—we're only human after all. You can accomplish this by focusing on your character and not your accomplishments. This is the first step to stopping being a perfectionist. Instead of striving for perfection and sometimes unrealistic goals, look at yourself in terms of who you are as a person—perhaps by exploring what values, beliefs, and passions drive you. This will help to create more balance in your life.

Allow mistakes to happen, as long as you learn from them there is no harm done. Perfectionists tend to be hard on themselves when they make errors—this can create anxiety, stress, and guilt which can lead to further procrastination. Making mistakes is part of life; it's how we learn and grow! Set reasonable goals and accept constructive criticism from those around you, such as friends or mentors who can offer guidance or advice.

Release the internal pressures that come with perfectionism—acknowledge that it's okay to be less than perfect. Don't procrastinate and then rush at the last minute—doing so will only increase your stress levels and make it harder for you to do a good job. If you need help managing your time or tasks, try breaking them down into small manageable chunks.

Remove negative influences from your life such as people who always expect perfection from you or belittle your efforts when things don't turn out perfectly—the support around you needs to be positive in order for self-growth and improvement. Try seeing the bigger picture—while details are important, it's also important to take an overall view of what's going on rather than simply focusing on the act itself. Lastly, adjust your standards by taking note of how much pressure you put on yourself. If it's too high, then adjust accordingly so that it's more realistic and manageable while still challenging enough for personal growth.

FORGIVENESS WORKSHEETS

There are four phases to the forgiving process: uncover, decision, work, and deepening. During each phase, it is important to use forgiveness worksheets to aid in the process by helping you uncover underlying issues, make conscious decisions about how to forgive, develop ways to work through difficult emotions and thoughts and deepen your forgiveness practice.

Part One: Uncovering Phase

The uncovering phase involves taking a deep look at your relationship with your inner child, exploring any underlying issues that may prevent you from forgiving yourself, and uncovering any limiting beliefs that may hold you back from the realization of your highest potential. Follow the prompts below to discover more about your inner child and your relationship with them.

What pain or turmoil have you faced? What were the most harmful aspects of the situation? How was the situation unfair? What was the root cause of your pain? Was it an external factor or something within you? Explain the problem in detail.

How did the situation make you feel? How did it affect you? For instance, did you experience painful emotions or distorted thinking?

....

....

....

....

Part Two: Decision

For this section, you will determine what forgiveness is for you and if you're willing to accept it. Think about the answers to the questions asked in part one, then answer the prompts below.

What does forgiveness mean to you? What does it look like in practice?

....

....

....

....

....

....

Pros and Cons

Make a pros and cons list of forgiving the person who harmed you. On one side, list the advantages of forgiving yourself and on the other, list potential risks.

Pros	Cons

Reflect On Forgiveness

Before deciding on whether to forgive the other person, describe how life or the situation might be different if you do forgive.

....

....

....

....

....

....

Are you willing to forgive yourself or others involved in the situation? Why or why not?

....

....

....

....

....

....

Part Three: Work

In this section, you will view the situation from the perspective of the offender. The goal is to gain a better understanding and empathy for what happened. What was the offender's experience? Put yourself in their shoes, seeing the world from their perspective and understanding what motivated them to make the choices they did. How was their childhood growing up? Could that have affected their behavior? What was their experience like during the offense?

....

....

....

Part Four: Deepening

The final stage involves developing a deep understanding and forgiveness of the person who wronged you. Take a moment to consider how forgiveness has improved your life. Has it improved your mental health? Has it allowed you to move forward in life? What has been the most meaningful part of your forgiveness journey?

What have you learned from the wrongdoings you suffered and choosing to forgive? Finally, take a moment to reflect on what you have learned from the inner child work and how it has changed your outlook. What are the ways you can practice self-compassion and forgiveness in the future? How will this help you lead a more fulfilling life?

By completing these exercises, you are taking an important step toward a healthier and happier you. By completing all four phases of the forgiving process, you can move forward in life and benefit from the healing power of forgiveness.

CHAPTER

8

FURTHER WORKSHEETS AND ACTIVITIES FOR HELPING YOUR INNER CHILD THRIVE

As we reviewed earlier in the book, although you can work through inner child issues and heal your inner child on your own, it's beneficial to use activities and worksheets to help you along. Additionally, you will likely continue to face trials and tribulations that may require further healing of your inner child or proper management techniques. This chapter provides resources and activities that can help you continue working toward inner peace and harmony.

20+ INNER CHILD HEALING EXERCISES

Healing your inner child doesn't only have to include journal prompts and reflection time. You can connect and heal using a variety of activities. Below are a few additional ways you can heal your inner child.

- Read an easy book from childhood: Whether it's a Dr. Seuss book, something from Disney, or any other classic children's literature that brings up happy memories, spend some time reading and enjoying a book from your childhood.

- Create an inner child scrapbook: Look through old photos, cards, drawings, and other memorabilia to put together a scrapbook of your younger years. This can help you remember all the good times that have been forgotten over the years.

- Write a letter: Sit down and write a letter to your inner child, reassuring them that they are loved, appreciated, and supported.

- Create a safe space: Create a physical or mental space where your inner child can go to feel secure and loved. This could be as a blanket fort, a virtual space in your mind, or anything else that makes you feel safe and at home.

- Relearn to play: Take some time to rediscover the joys of play. Whether it's playing tag with friends, playing an instrument, drawing pictures, or just goofing around with no agenda, remember to enjoy the simple pleasures of childhood.

- Watch your favorite childhood movie or show: Indulging in some of your childhood favorites can help to bring back memories and remind you of a happier time in life.

- Visit a playground: Visit the park, playgrounds, or anywhere else that makes you feel like a kid again. Jump on the swings, climb up the monkey bars, and just have fun!

- Daydream: Take some time to imagine and daydream, just like you used to. Let your imagination run wild, explore different worlds, and dream of the possibilities.

- Remember the little things: Reflect on the little moments that made childhood so special. Those small details can often tell bigger stories. Think about the sounds, smells, and feelings that defined your childhood.

- Have a slumber party: Have a slumber party with friends or family, and just enjoy being silly. Share stories, watch movies, and have some snacks.

- Write childhood memories: Sit down and write out some of your fondest childhood memories to remind yourself of the joys that life can bring when we simply embrace our inner child.

- Rediscover an old pastime: Dig up an old hobby or activity you used to enjoy as a child and take some time to do it again. Whether it's building model planes, playing video games, or something else entirely, make sure to have fun!

- Play with chalk, bubbles, or other outdoor toys: On a nice day, go outside and play with some classic outdoor toys like chalk, bubbles, or other childhood favorites. This can help you remember the feeling of being carefree and happy.

- Paint a picture: Paint a painting that brings to life all the things your inner child loves and adores. Use bright colors, abstract shapes, and whatever else makes you feel at home.

- Go to a carnival: Find a nearby carnival or amusement park and take some time to enjoy the rides, games, and shows. A carnival is an awesome way to tap into your inner child.

- Throw an ice cream party: Indulging in an ice cream party with friends or family is an awesome way to enjoy some sweet treats and share childhood memories.

- Sing your favorite childhood songs: You can sing along to some of your favorite childhood songs to connect with your inner child—and the sillier, the better! Whether it's nursery rhymes, Disney songs, or something else entirely, let yourself get lost in the music.

- Hug and kiss a teddy bear: No matter how old you are, it's always nice to hug and kiss your favorite teddy bear. This can help remind you of the love and comfort that comes with childhood.

- Complete a puzzle, craft, or other indoor activity: These activities can be a great way to bring back the feeling of accomplishment and help you relax.

- Express your feelings in a tactile way: If you don't feel like talking, express your feelings with a tactile activity. This can include creative activities like drawing, painting, playing with clay, or any other way to connect with your inner child.

- Play pretend: Take some time to play pretend—dress up as your favorite character or imagine yourself in a different world. Let your imagination run wild and transport yourself back to the days of childhood.

- Let go: Take a moment to let go of any worries or doubts, and just enjoy the present moment. Relax, smile, and be happy—just like a child would.

- Be unfiltered: Remind yourself of the importance of being present and open to new experiences. Don't be restrained by social norms or what is expected of you—allow yourself to just be.

These are just a few ideas for helping your inner child thrive. Incorporating some of these activities into your daily routine can make all the difference in reconnecting with and nurturing your inner child. With practice, you will rediscover the wonder and joy that comes.

SUPPORTING AND LOVING POSITIVE AFFIRMATIONS

One of the most powerful tools for healing your inner child is positive affirmations. Affirmations allow you to address your inner child and create positive, supportive statements to help bring about healing. They work by helping you find a new, more positive story to tell yourself and override any limiting beliefs or negative self-talk that may have been instilled during childhood. Here are some affirmations you can use to start healing your inner child:

- I am deeply loved and accepted for who I am.

- There is something special about me and it deserves to be celebrated.

- I am worthy of my own love and care no matter what happens in life.

- I have the power to create positive changes in my life with my own thoughts, words, and actions.

- I can find peace within myself by trusting my emotions and being patient with myself during times of difficulty.

- I choose to understand that the past does not define me and that moving forward is the only way to reach true inner child healing and growth.

- It is okay for me to make mistakes, as this is part of learning, growing, and developing into a better version of myself each day.

- I release all judgment of myself that has been hindering my progress and focus on loving, nurturing, accepting, and supporting myself instead so that I can flourish as an individual in all areas of life.

- My mistakes are only a stepping stone toward success; they do not define or limit who I am today or who I can become in the future.

- No matter what comes my way or how difficult things may seem at first, there will always be goodness ahead if I choose to stay focused on staying true to myself while remaining open-minded to new ideas and opportunities for growth along the way.

- I embrace change as it offers me new ways to learn more about myself so that I can move forward in an empowered mindset rather than feeling stuck in fear or regret from prior experiences.

- I allow room for creativity by exploring different paths life offers me without being held back with negative beliefs about my potential.

- I understand taking risks leads to self-discovery: no matter what comes out of it, it will help me grow wiser.

- It is okay for me to take time off from anything causing stress: doing this helps build resilience so that when faced with struggles again later on down the road , they won't be quite as formidable.

- My worthiness is unconditional: no person or situation can take away its power unless given permission by me.

- I come alive when pursuing passions: whether through hobbies or professional pursuits; I appreciate what ignites a fire within my soul.

- I honor all parts of myself—both strengths and weaknesses—equally so that balance can be achieved between them.

- No matter how terrible the situation may seem right now, there is something beautiful waiting around every corner—even if it takes searching, finding it will provide a sense of peace and comfort.

- The power lies within me; by believing this truth, any difficult situation can be faced with courage and confidence instead of fear and anxiety.

- My thoughts are powerful beyond measure; therefore, bringing awareness into them allows them to become conscious enough for transformation and inner child healing efforts.

- I am enough. Every day, I am growing into the person I want to be and becoming better than yesterday.

- I believe in myself and my own potential. No matter what happens, I will never give up on myself or my dreams.

- I trust that all of my experiences have helped me grow and become stronger.

- It's ok to make mistakes and learn from them, it's how we grow and become smarter and wiser each day.

- When life gets tough, I look within myself for strength to get through it because I know that resilience is a powerful skill of mine that can't be taken away from me.

- I can achieve anything that I set my mind to with perseverance, dedication, hard work, and determination.

- I forgive myself because progress isn't linear; instead, it's made up of ups and downs, which are just as important for growth as the successes themselves are!

- My inner child is filled with creative ideas and feelings that have yet to be explored—by nurturing this part of myself, I can make these ideas come to life!

- No matter what kind of struggles come my way, they do not define who I am or who I am on the inside; rather they serve as opportunities for personal development so that the victorious version of me can emerge at the end!

SELF-ACCEPTANCE WORKSHEETS FOR THE WOUNDED INNER CHILD

Your Life Vision

Inner child work is all about self-discovery and healing. Start by creating a vision for your life, including what kind of person you want to be, what relationships and experiences you want to have, and what kind of legacy you want to leave. Pretend that there is nothing standing in your way. Money, time, and resources are not an issue. What do you want your life to look like?

_____

_____

_____

_____

_____

_____

_____

_____

_____

_____

_____

_____

_____

_____

_____

Distorted and Automatic Thought Challenger

Inner child work is also about challenging the distorted and automatic thoughts that keep us from making changes in our lives. As adults, we may be unaware of how deep these negative thought patterns go back to our childhoods. Take some time to write down all the ways you think negatively about yourself and your life. Then challenge those negatives with more positive and realistic thoughts. An example is done for you below.

Stressor or trigger	Distorted thought	Challenge	New thoughts
Doing poorly at an interview and not getting the job.	I'm a complete failure.	What proves that I'm a complete failure? Doing poorly at one job interview does not mean I'm a failure. Everyone fails sometimes.	While I may not be very successful or have achieved all my goals yet, I'm still a worthy and capable person. Everyone goes through tough times and setbacks in life, this is just one of them.

It's Time • Heal Your Inner Child and Come Back Home

Inner Child Mirror Exercise

The inner child mirror exercise helps you to recognize the parts of yourself that need healing. To begin, stand in front of a mirror and bring your attention to your reflection. Ask yourself: What does my inner child need today? Notice any physical sensations or emotions that come up for you during this exercise. With one hand on your heart and the other on your belly, sit with these feelings for a few minutes.

Next, imagine that you are looking into the eyes of your inner child in the mirror. Take a few moments to appreciate all the parts of yourself that makeup who you are today. With an open heart and mind, ask yourself what message does my inner child need to hear? Write down your answer on the lined space below. Finally, write a few affirmations for yourself related to this message and repeat them out loud or in your head as you look into the mirror. Take your time with this exercise and take in all the love that surrounds you. When you are ready, slowly come back into the present moment.

Understanding Your Inner Child's Perspective

Your inner child can act out at the worst times, and it's difficult to understand why. This exercise will help you gain a better perspective of your inner child's needs and wants.

To begin, take two chairs and have them face one another. One chair represents your inner child. Sit in it and take a few deep breaths. Imagine yourself as your younger self and note if you feel any physical sensations or emotions. Now, allow your inner child to explain their feelings and needs.

After they are done speaking, switch to the other chair and respond as your present self. As an adult, we are more rational and able to empathize differently than our inner child. Keep switching back and forth until your inner child is done expressing themselves. When finished, thank your inner child and bid them a fond farewell. Take some time to reflect on what was said in the space below.

....

....

....

....

....

Cultivating Acceptance Meditation

For this exercise, you will meditate to cultivate acceptance of your inner child. Start by finding a comfortable seated position and closing your eyes, allowing yourself to relax into the present moment and noticing your breath. Bring your attention to the physical sensations in your body and allow yourself to be with them without judgment.

Next, think of some negative beliefs your parents or caregivers may have expressed to you during your childhood. For example, did they tell you "You're not smart enough," or "You should be ashamed of yourself"? Notice any feelings that come up and allow them to pass through you.

Did you become tense? How does your body feel? Lower your shoulders from your ears, and allow yourself to let go. Take a few deep breaths and surrender any judgments you have about yourself.

Now, imagine your inner child standing in front of you and repeating a few affirming statements such as "I'm safe," or "I'm enough." Repeat this several times, speaking each phrase slowly and deliberately. As you do so, open your arms and welcome your inner child into your embrace. Feel the warmth of being accepted, and feel the release of tension and pain. When you are ready, slowly open your eyes.

Inner child work can be challenging, but it's also very rewarding. By taking the time to connect to your inner child, you can learn to understand yourself better and heal from any unresolved issues from the past.

10+ FUN ACTIVITIES TO CONNECT TO YOUR INNER CHILD

In addition to using positive affirmations, there are many other activities you can engage in to help your inner child thrive. Here are 10 fun activities to get you started:

- Get messy: Put on some old clothes and make a mess with paints, flour, mud—whatever you have handy! Get creative and let your inner child come out to play!

- Make a fort: Grab some sheets and blankets and create your own little world. It can be an indoor tent or a castle in the garden, it doesn't matter as long as you can find some peace and quiet for yourself.

- Play with toys: Get out your old toys, board games or anything that brings back happy memories. Remember how much fun it was to play? Allow yourself to relax and have some fun!

- Move your body: Dance, jump, or hop like a child and let go of all inhibitions. Feel the joy in movement.

- Hang out with kids: Spend time with kids who are around you—your siblings, friends' children, or neighbors. Let them take the lead and follow their playful energy.

- Be destructive: In a safe way, of course! Break some twigs in the park and have fun with sticks and stones. Breaking things can be entertaining and it's a great way to relieve stress.

- Look at your baby photos: Take a look at photos of yourself as a baby and see how much you've grown since then. This can help to remind you of your innocence and how much potential there is within you.

- Make your favorite meal from childhood: Think about what your favorite meals were when you were younger and make one for yourself. Eating can be a wonderful way to reconnect with our inner child and bring back happy memories.

- Reconnect with an old friend: Reach out to an old friend and make plans to meet up. There's nothing like catching up with someone who knew you before the world got complicated and confusing.

- Dance in the rain: There's something so liberating about dancing in the rain and letting go of all your worries. Feel the drops on your skin, splash around in puddles, and enjoy the moment.

- Go stargazing and wish upon a star: Gaze at the stars in the night sky and make a wish. Let your imagination take you away and experience the beauty of the universe.

SELF-COMPASSION WORKSHEETS

Releasing Old Emotions

Sometimes our inner child is holding onto old, unresolved emotions such as fear, anger, sadness, and shame. Take some time to recognize the source of these emotions and what they were trying to tell you. Then sit with them and allow yourself to release them by writing out your story or using affirmations. Make sure to be gentle and understanding with yourself throughout this process.

Childhood Timeline

Starting from your earliest memory and on to adulthood (stop at age 21 if older), create a timeline of your life. Note down all the major events and experiences that have affected you—anything you deem "important." Then review the timeline, reflecting on the lessons you've learned and how these experiences shaped who you are today. Do you notice any common themes or patterns? What can you do to move forward with a healthier outlook?

....

....

....

....

....

....

....

....

Interview With Your Inner Child

For this exercise, you will take some time to sit down and "talk" with your inner child. To prepare for your interview, first, create a list of questions you'd like to ask your inner child. These can be positive, negative, or neutral. Below are example questions to get you started.

- What do you need right now?

- What were some of your happiest memories as a child?

- Are there any secrets you'd like to tell me?

- What do you wish I could have done differently for you?

....

....

....

....

....

....

Once your list is complete, place a chair in front of you and imagine your inner child seated in it. Then take turns asking and answering the questions. Write down any insights that come up during this process. Listen to the internal responses and sensations with an open heart and mind. Above all, be kind to yourself throughout the inner child work process and remember that it's a journey. Remind yourself that no matter what, you can always start again.

Rewrite Your Painful Memories

Sometimes our most painful memories can be hard to let go of. To help you do this, try rewriting your painful memories into something more positive and empowering. Using the lined space below, write down the memory that is causing you pain.

Next, rewrite the memory in a way that it no longer causes you pain—focus on the positive aspects of the experience. It can be helpful to think of this exercise as creating a story for your inner child with a happy ending. This could look like changing the outcome or replacing a negative label with something more empowering. When you are finished, read the new story to yourself and take a moment to feel the transformation in your energy. You can also write down some affirmations related to this memory and use them when needed for further healing.

Nurture Your Innerself

For this exercise, you will need several photos of your younger self. It helps to have three to six photos from varying ages. Place the photos in front of you and take a few moments to observe each photo. Pay attention to how your mind and body react. Do you remember yourself during those moments?

Now, pick up a photo and look into the eyes of your younger self. Tell them all the things that you needed to hear as a child. This could look like, "I love you", "you are enough", or "it is okay to make mistakes." Speak these words out loud or in your head and take some time to feel the healing that comes with each phrase. After you finish with one photo, move on to the next. When you are finished, take a few moments to appreciate yourself and give thanks for all you have achieved. Use the space below to reflect on your experience.

Affirming Your Inner Child

For this exercise, first create a list of friends, family, mentors—anyone who makes you feel safe and loved. Once your list is complete, write down loving and compassionate phrases that each of these people would say to you. Add some of your own or change them to be more suitable for the present you.

....

....

....

....

Next, sit in a comfortable position and bring your attention to your inner child. Take a few deep breaths and imagine that the people you listed slowly began to surround your inner child. Visualize each of them speaking the words you wrote down. When one person is done, the next takes their place and continues to shower your inner child with love and support. When you are ready, bring yourself back to the present moment.

....

....

....

....

....

....

It is important to remember that inner child work is about healing and not about perfection. Be gentle with yourself and take time to give yourself the love and support you deserve.

Non-Dominant Hand Activity

Using our non-dominant hand can activate different parts of the brain that may be associated with the inner child. For this activity, grab a separate notebook and pen. You will switch back and forth between your dominant and nondominant hand as you write. Using your dominant hand and the corresponding page (e.g., left-hand and left page), write positive affirmations about yourself. Think of words and phrases that describe your strengths, successes, and accomplishments.

When finished, switch to your non-dominant hand and the other page. Allow it to do whatever is comfortable. You can write, draw, scribble—there are no wrong answers. This is a great way for your inner child to express themselves in a safe and creative way. Then switch back to your dominant hand and respond in a compassionate and loving way. Keep switching back and forth until your inner child is ready to stop.

Strengthening Your Adult Self

Compared to children, adults have the advantage of being more logical and rational and can be daring. By strengthening your adult self and understanding how your inner child works, you can help your inner child to heal and grow. For this exercise, you will create your own toolbox full of facts and arguments for you to use to challenge distorted beliefs and negative behavior. Take some time to write down different strategies you can use to confront irrational thoughts or feelings. A few examples of facts and arguments are prepared below.

- Everyone has flaws, and that's okay.

- It is normal to feel scared or anxious sometimes.

- Taking risks can lead to glorious rewards.

When your toolbox is complete, take a few moments to thank yourself for the work you have done and congratulate yourself for being so courageous.

By completing the exercises in this chapter, you have taken an important step toward healing your inner child and creating a better relationship with yourself. Through self-care, inner child work, and understanding your own perspective, you are better able to heal the past wounds and create a stronger and more compassionate relationship with your inner child.

JOURNALING PROMPTS

Writing can be a powerful tool for healing, and there are many journaling prompts you can use to work through issues related to your inner child. Below are some prompts to help you further your healing.

How can you nurture your inner child? What activities can you do to reignite their spark and re-energize them? Is there anything that can help them feel safe, accepted, and validated?

What does your inner child need to learn? Consider what lessons or skills your inner child needs to develop. What values can you teach them to help them grow and develop their confidence? How can you create a safe environment for them to explore and learn?

Consider what advice you'd give to your inner child if they could hear you. What words of wisdom would encourage and inspire them? What tips would help guide them through difficult times?

Recall your favorite toys and activities as a child, and why they were so important to you. How did these toys or activities make you feel? What did they teach you and how have these lessons stayed with you?

Name an object or experience you were grateful for as a child. What did it teach you about life? How did it affect the way you view the world? What lessons can you take from this experience and how can it help shape who you are today?

Did you feel connected to your family or friends growing up? Reflect on your relationships with family and friends as a child. How did these relationships shape the person you are today? What lessons can you learn from these relationships and how can they help you heal?

Write down the top five phrases your inner child needs to hear or the top five phrases you wish you could tell yourself as a child.

Describe your childhood bedroom and what it meant to you. How do you think that connects to who you are today? How would an adult redecorate the room for your inner child?

What are the boundaries or limits that you set for yourself as a child and how have they changed?

What are some of the biggest lessons or takeaways you've learned as an adult that could have benefited your inner child?

Finally, reflect on how you can use the knowledge and wisdom from your inner child to live a more fulfilled life. How can you tap into their perspective and use it to create a life of joy and happiness?

Write two letters—neither of them will be sent (unless you wish) so be honest, raw, and open. The first letter will be for the caregivers or parents who influenced your early childhood. Name, at most, five experiences that may have harmed or hindered you from feeling safe and loved. Then see if you can list at least five positive and nurturing experiences you learned from them.

The second letter is for your inner child. Apologize for the listed burdens and hardships you faced and thank them for the resilience, creativity, and courage they have developed. Let them know you are here for them and will do your best to protect them. Assure them that you are committed to giving them the love, trust, and playfulness they deserve.

Then name at least five things you would like to say and do differently now as an adult to make them feel truly cherished, empowered, and accepted.

This activity will help you acknowledge and make peace with the past while learning to trust, love, and play in the present. Through this process, you will learn how to embrace the inner child within and regain the joy and wonder of childhood.

As a child, what did you worry about and why? Did you experience anxiety or fear and how did it shape you? Reflect on the worries that were a part of your childhood, why they mattered to you, and how they may still affect you today. How can understanding these anxieties help you foster a sense of self-love and acceptance?

Write about a situation where you felt misunderstood or unheard as a child. Describe how this experience made you feel, what it taught you, and why it still matters today. How can understanding these experiences help you cultivate self-compassion and support the needs of your inner child?

Consider which parenting attributes you like and dislike. If you have a child(ren) or plan to in the future, what do you want to replicate, and which will you want to avoid? How can understanding your own upbringing help you become a better parent?

Take some time to think about which activities or hobbies you loved as a child. Is it something you still enjoy today, or have you let it go? How can you incorporate these activities into your life once more and why is this important for your inner child?

Reflect on the impact of relationships, such as teachers, siblings, and best friends on your development. How did these connections shape you and the way you view yourself? What can you learn about loving, trusting, and playing in relationships today?

Write down a list of ten things that make you feel happy and relaxed. Choose five of these to focus on for the next week and notice how they make you feel.

Reflect on a positive memory from childhood that makes you smile. Describe the scene, people, and emotions involved in this memory. What are you grateful for and how can you bring more of these experiences into your life?

These are all questions and activities you can use to help you reconnect with your inner child, learn to trust and love yourself, and regain the childlike wonder. By building a secure relationship with your inner child, you can tap into their perspective and create a life of joy, spontaneity, and resilience.

CONCLUSION

My close friend, Grace, never thought she would grapple with her inner child. She had always seemed so confident and in control on the outside, but deep down within her heart, she was struggling. Her inner child represented the part of her that had been neglected and hurt, and it had taken a toll on her emotionally.

When Grace was a little girl, her parents were divorced, leaving her feeling abandoned and alone. Her father rarely came around to visit, leaving most of the parenting duties up to her mother. As Grace grew older, she began to feel like a burden—like no matter how hard she tried she could never be good enough for either parent. This made it difficult for Grace to form relationships as an adult because she felt insecure about herself and always feared abandonment.

The emotions from this childhood trauma remained unresolved and began to manifest in Grace's adult life as anger outbursts whenever something didn't go her way or when someone hurt her feelings. Even though these episodes weren't directed at anyone else but herself, they left Grace feeling drained and exhausted afterward.

Grace realized that she needed help dealing with the issues from her past if she wanted to lead a happy life going forward. After many months of therapy sessions, journaling exercises, meditation practices, and regular self-care habits such as yoga classes—all focused on healing her inner child—she slowly started to make progress in resolving the emotional pain from her childhood trauma that had been driving her self-sabotaging behavior for so long.

Over time, Grace recognized where certain patterns of behavior stemmed from and were better able to manage them appropriately when they arose. With each passing day, grace found more peace within herself which allowed for healthier relationships with others where mutual trust and respect could blossom without fear of abandonment or criticism.

Most importantly, with the guidance of professionals, Grace learned how to give love back to that neglected part inside of herself that was still hurting after all these years—her inner child. Ultimately, this allowed for true transformation and lasting recovery from the trauma she'd experienced in childhood that had led to so much pain throughout adulthood too.

We all have an inner child to answer to. While some might be better behaved than others, all inner children need some love and attention from their adult selves in order to heal. Inner child work is a powerful tool that can help us understand ourselves better, learn to accept and nurture ourselves, and ultimately become happier, healthier, and more balanced individuals.

Here's a quick reminder of what you've learned:

- Acknowledge the existence of your inner child. Your inner child is a part of you and an important piece of who you are. Recognizing their presence helps give them a voice and allows for healing to occur.

- Create a safe space for yourself to explore and connect with your inner child. This can include meditating, journaling, or any other activity that puts you in touch with your feelings and emotions.

- Learn how to re-parent yourself. Give yourself the care, acceptance, understanding, and unconditional love that you are looking for from others but haven't been able to find in life yet. This includes being gentle, compassionate, forgiving, and non-judgmental with yourself.

- Tap into your emotions effectively and appropriately by allowing yourself to experience your emotions fully without judgment or criticism as they arise. This will help get in touch with how your inner child feels about certain situations or experiences in life.

- Heal your trauma appropriately. Healing trauma that has occurred in childhood and beyond is an essential step in inner child healing work, as it can be the root cause of many current issues we face today. This can include revisiting memories through visualization techniques, creative expression activities such as art or writing, or seeking guidance from a professional therapist if necessary.

- Invite healthy playfulness into your life. Playing is often associated with childhood and can help bring joy back into our lives when we integrate it back into our adult lives more often than not! Activities such as coloring books for adults, puzzles, and board games are all great ways to introduce playfulness into your life again!

- Process negative experiences in a healthy way. It's ok to feel angry at times or even to express those feelings constructively when needed! Taking time to process negative experiences from the past by expressing those feelings (perhaps through writing) will help clear old negative energy so it no longer holds us back from living our best lives now!

- Connect with your inner child. Spend quality time connecting with them by letting them know what positive attributes you appreciate about them or talking about things they like doing! This will help build trust between you two and strengthen your relationship so that healing may occur both on an external level but also internally.

Now that you have all the tools to heal and nurture your inner child, go out there and use them. As you embark on this journey of healing and self-discovery, you will come to understand more deeply the importance of taking care of yourself and the effects of neglecting your inner child. Healing your inner child is not a one-time effort but a continuous effort that requires dedication, patience, and self-compassion.

If you have enjoyed this book and found it helpful in your journey toward healing yourself, please take a few moments to leave a review on Amazon. Give details about why this book was effective in helping you heal your inner child and any insights gained from the advice given. Your words may help others who are struggling to find healing for themselves. We thank you for your support!

SPECIAL BONUS!

WANT A FREE BOOK?

**GET FREE UNLIMITED ACCESS TO THIS BOOK
AND ALL MY NEW BOOKS BY JOINING MY
FAN BASE !**

SCAN QR CODE--->

REFERENCES

Ackerman, C. E. (2018, August 6). *What is Self-Expression and How to Foster It? (20 Activities + Examples)*. PositivePsychology.com. https://positivepsychology.com/self-expression/

Ali, A. (2021, October 7). *8 Signs You Are Carrying A Wounded Inner Child Within!* The Easy Wisdom. https://theeasywisdom.com/signs-you-have-a-wounded-inner-child-quiz/?amp=1

Aurel, M. (2022, June 28). *How To Use The Psychological Concept Of The Inner Child To Make Better Business Decisions*. Forbes. https://www.forbes.com/sites/forbesbusinesscouncil/2022/06/28/how-to-use-the-psychological-concept-of-the-inner-child-to-make-better-business-decisions/amp/

Authenticity Worksheet.pdf. (n.d.). Dropbox. https://www.dropbox.com/s/c9pg6f7atnzxvq5/Authenticity%20Worksheet.pdf?dl=0

Azman, T., & Tsabary, S. (2022, July 18). *Conscious Parenting Isn't About Your Child, But Your Inner Child*. Mindvalley Blog. https://blog.mindvalley.com/conscious-parenting/amp/

Best 15 Inner Child Healing Exercises To Reparent Your Inner Child (+ FREE Inner Child Worksheets). (2022, September 8). Ineffable Living. https://ineffableliving.com/inner-child-exercises/

BetterHelp Editorial Team. (2022, October 6). *Inner Child: What Is It, What Happened To It, And How Can I Fix It? | Betterhelp*. Www.betterhelp.com. https://www.betterhelp.com/advice/therapy/inner-child-what-is-it-what-happened-to-it-and-how-can-i-fix-it/

Brenner, G. H. (2017, May 25). *12 Keys To A Great Self-Relationship, Starting Now | Psychology Today*. Www.psychologytoday.com. https://www.psychologytoday.com/us/blog/experimentations/201705/12-keys-great-self-relationship-starting-now?amp

Broadway, K. (2016, November 7). *9 Ways to Self-Parent*. Katherinebroadway. https://www.raleighpsychotherapy.com/single-post/2016/10/31/9-ways-to-self-parent

Byrne, D. (n.d.). *Self-Care: Accepting Ourselves For Who Truly Are. (Including Worksheets) How do you regain your acceptance of yourself?* https://deborah-byrnepsychologyservices.com/wp-content/uploads/2020/03/Accepting-Ourselves-For-Who-Truly-Are-Including-Worksheets.pdf

Carnahan, L. (2021, December 1). *Love Yourself First: What Does It Really Mean and How Do You Do It?* The Vector Impact by Vector Marketing. https://www.thevectorimpact.com/love-yourself-first/

Chen, L. (2015, October 19). *7 Things Your Inner Child Needs to Hear You Say*. Tiny Buddha. https://tinybuddha.com/blog/7-things-your-inner-child-needs-to-hear-you-say/

Choix, J. (n.d.). *How To Improve Your Relationships By Healing Your Inner Child Wounds*. Mywellbeing.com. https://mywellbeing.com/ask-a-therapist/improve-your-relationships

Christian, L. (2021a, February 22). *How to Trust Yourself: Building True Self-Confidence*. SoulSalt. https://soulsalt.com/how-to-trust-yourself/

Christian, L. (2021b, March 22). *How to Be Your Authentic Self: 7 Powerful Strategies to Be True*. SoulSalt. https://soulsalt.com/how-to-be-your-authentic-self/

Clements, W. (n.d.). *Understanding The Spiritual Connection With Your Inner Child*. https://winstonclements.com/understanding-the-spiritual-connection-with-your-inner-child/

Connell, L. K. (2022, June 8). *What Is Self-Parenting And How It's A Part of Healing*. Lifehack. https://www.lifehack.org/924532/self-parenting

Cooks-Campbell, A. (2022, March 15). *How Inner Child Work Enables Healing and Playful Discovery*. Www.betterup.com. https://www.betterup.com/blog/inner-child-work

Davis, A. (2023, January 3). *20+ Inner Child Activities to Heal and Feel Alive - Ambitiously Alexa*. Ambitiously Alexa. https://ambitiouslyalexa.com/inner-child-activities/

DeSanctis, E. (2018, March 30). *The Importance of Having a Healthy Relationship With Yourself*. One Love Foundation. https://www.joinonelove.org/learn/the-importance-of-having-a-healthy-relationship-with-yourself/

Dienstman, A. M. (2020, November 26). *7 Ways to Reconnect with Your Inner Child*. Goodnet. https://www.goodnet.org/articles/7-ways-to-reconnect-your-inner-child

Digging up the past: Helpful or harmful? (2018, October 10). Insight Counselling. https://www.insightcounselling.com.hk/blog/digging-up-the-past-helpful-or-harmful

Edwards, N. (n.d.). *5 Ways to Maintain a Healthy Relationship with Yourself*. Happify.com. https://www.happify.com/hd/5-ways-to-maintain-a-healthy-relationship-with-yourself/

Elisheva. (2021, May 19). *Inner child work: how your past affects your present and what you can do*. Lionhearted Counseling LLC. https://lionheartedcounseling.com/inner-child-work-how-your-past-affects-your-present-and-what-you-can-do/

Esposito, L. (2018, April 30). *Learning to Parent Yourself as an Adult | Psychology Today*. Www.psychologytoday.com. https://www.psychologytoday.com/us/blog/anxiety-zen/201804/learning-parent-yourself-adult?amp

Goldstein, E. (n.d.). *What Is An Inner Child | And What Does It Know — Integrative Psychotherapy Mental Health Blog*. Integrative Psychotherapy & Trauma Treatment. https://integrativepsych.co/new-blog/what-is-an-inner-child

GoodTherapy.org Staff. (2014, October 8). *The Psychology of Trust Issues and Ways to Overcome Them - GoodTherapy.org Therapy Blog*. Www.goodtherapy.org. https://www.goodtherapy.org/blog/the-psychology-of-trust-issues-and-ways-to-overcome-them/amp/

GoodTherapy.org Staff. (2016, August 29). *15 Tips for Letting Go of a Relationship That Is Not Healthy*. Www.goodtherapy.org. https://www.goodtherapy.org/blog/15-tips-for-letting-go-of-a-relationship-that-is-not-healthy-0829167/amp/

Grille, R. (2015, February 1). *Inner Child, Inner Wisdom: Unmasking The Mythology Of The Modern, Uber Parent.* Kindred Media. https://kindredmedia. org/2015/02/parenting-heros-journey-unmasking-mythology-modern-uber-parent/

Harvard Health Publishing. (2019). *4 ways to boost your self-compassion.* Harvard Health; Harvard Health. https://www.health.harvard.edu/mental-health/4-ways-to-boost-your-self-compassion

Heflick, N. A. (2014, September 21). *The Psychology of "YOLO."* Www.psychologytoday.com. https://www.psychologytoday.com/us/blog/the-big-questions/201309/the-psychology-yolo?amp

The Hormona Team. (2020, July 7). *Your inner child: Time to heal them.* Hormona. https://www.hormona.io/your-inner-child-what-why-important/

Is Your Inner Child Hurting? Ten Signs To Check – Psychotherapy, Counselling, Hypnotherapy with Malminder Gill at Harley Street, London. (n.d.). Hypnosis in London. https://www.hypnosis-in-london.com/is-your-inner-child-hurting-ten-signs-to-check/

J., L. (2021, April 8). *The art of self-expression.* In Education Online. https://ineducationonline.org/2021/04/08/the-art-of-self-expression/

Jay. (2022, November 6). *How to be your authentic self: 11 Strategies to be your true self.* Mind by Design. https://www.mindbydesign.io/authentic-self/

Kaplan, E. (2016, October 18). *Why Unleashing Your Inner Child Will Make You Insanely Creative, According to Science.* Mission.org. https://medium.com/the-mission/how-acting-like-a-5-year-old-will-make-you-insanely-creative-and-successful-according-to-science-a0ff48283a98

Kitazawa, E. (2022, August 28). *6 Causes of Inner Child Wounds (+Their Effects).* Shortform Books. https://www.shortform.com/blog/inner-child-wounds/

Knight, R. (2019, April 29). *How to Manage Your Perfectionism.* Harvard Business Review. https://hbr.org/2019/04/how-to-manage-your-perfectionism

Kristenson, S. (2022a, January 16). *How to Reparent Yourself: A 7-Step Guide*. Happier Human. https://www.happierhuman.com/reparent-yourself/

Kristenson, S. (2022b, October 11). *13 Signs You're Dealing with Inner Childhood Wounds*. Happier Human. https://www.happierhuman.com/inner-child-hood-wounds/

Letting Go of the False Self. (2019, March 24). Thrive Mind. https://www.thrivemindquantumcoaching.com/jenny-dawson-blog/2019/3/24/letting-go-of-the-false-self

Lim, E. (2022, January 3). *How to Validate Your Inner Child with What to Say*. Abundance Coach for Women in Business | Evelyn Lim. https://www.evelynlim.com/how-to-validate-your-inner-child/

Livia. (2022, January 25). *22 Ways to Connect With Your Inner Child - Made With Lemons*. Madewithlemons.co. https://madewithlemons.co/connect-with-your-inner-child/

Lo, I. (2019, July 24). *4 Ways to Release Anger Towards Your Parents*. Www.psychologytoday.com. https://www.psychologytoday.com/us/blog/living-emotional-intensity/201907/4-ways-release-anger-to-wards-your-parents?amp

Lopy, I. (n.d.). *"So, I Quit" - Why stripping away your False Self is the best way forward*. Eggshell Therapy and Coaching. https://eggshelltherapy.com/freearticles/2018/02/28/so-i-quit/

Louise, A. (2022, February 22). *The number one reason to heal your past and why you may not want to*. Life Coach & Mentor. https://www.getreal.lu/one-reason-to-heal-your-past/

Lynnefisher. (2016, September 25). *Find Your Inner Child To Free Your Creativity and Nurture Your Spirit*. Head to Head, Heart to Heart. https://lynnefisher.wordpress.com/2016/09/25/inner-child-creativity-spirit/

Lyons, M. (2021, September 7). *Being Your Authentic Self Is Easier Said than Done but Worth It*. Www.betterup.com. https://www.betterup.com/blog/authentic-self?hs_amp=true#hard-to-be

M. L. K. Support. (2021, November 3). *Read About How to living with a wounded inner child*. Blissiree. https://blissiree.com/are-you-living-with-a-wounded-inner-child/

Manu Melwin Joy. (2014, April 20). *Integrated adult - Transactional Analysis.* Slide Share. https://www.slideshare.net/manumjoy/integrated-adult

Marissa. (2022, June 11). *7 Signs You're an Authentic Person - Inside and Out!* A to Zen Life. https://atozenlife.com/authentic-person/

Mhlungu, G. (2020, February 20). *How to parent yourself.* Bona Magazine. https://www.bona.co.za/love/how-to-parent-yourself/

Michael, C. (2022, February 15). *10 Signs you have a Wounded Inner Child Impacting your Relationships.* Elephant Journal | Daily Blog, Videos, E-Newsletter & Magazine on Yoga + Organics + Green Living + Non-New Agey Spirituality + Ecofashion + Conscious Consumerism=It's about the Mindful Life. https://www.elephantjournal.com/2022/02/is-your-wounded-inner-child-impacting-your-relationships/

Mind Tools Content Team. (n.d.). *Authenticity.* Www.mindtools.com. https://www.mindtools.com/ay30irc/authenticity

Modern Therapy. (n.d.). *Self-Apologies: How to Heal Shame & Guilt Through Self-Forgiveness.* Moderntherapy.online. https://moderntherapy.online/blog-2/2021/3/15/self-apologies-how-to-heal-shame-amp-guilt-through-self-forgiveness?format=amp

My Online Therapy. (2021, March 26). *What is your inner child (and why it's important you get to know them).* My Online Therapy. https://myonlinetherapy.com/what-is-your-inner-child-and-why-its-important-you-get-to-know-them/

Oregon Counseling. (2021, April 15). *10 Ways to Overcome Perfectionism.* Oregon Counseling. https://oregoncounseling.com/article/10-ways-to-overcome-perfectionism/

Pattemore, C. (2021, June 3). *10 Ways to Build and Preserve Better Boundaries.* Psych Central. https://psychcentral.com/lib/10-way-to-build-and-preserve-better-boundaries

Pikörn, I. (2019, August 30). *Noticing, Healing and Freeing Your Inner Child.* Insight Timer Blog. https://insighttimer.com/blog/inner-child-meaning-noticing-healing-freeing/

Raab, D. (2018, August 6). *Deep Secrets and Inner Child Healing | Psychology Today.* Www.psychologytoday.com. https://www.psychologytoday.com/us/

blog/the-empowerment-diary/201808/deep-secrets-and-inner-child-healing?amp

Raman, L. (2015, March 17). *Letting Go of Toxic Relationships and Rediscovering Yourself*. Tiny Buddha. https://tinybuddha.com/blog/letting-go-of-un-healthy-relationships-and-rediscovering-yourself/

Raypole, C. (2020, July 8). *8 Tips for Healing Your Inner Child*. Healthline. https://www.healthline.com/health/mental-health/inner-child-healing

Raypole, C. (2022, August 24). *Guilt Makes a Heavy Burden. Don't Let It Drag You Down*. Healthline. https://www.healthline.com/health/mental-health/how-to-stop-feeling-guilty#signs

Robbins, M. (2021, October 25). *The Importance of Self-Trust*. Mike-Robbins.com. https://mike-robbins.com/the-importance-of-self-trust/

says, T. (2022, January 25). *22 Ways to Connect With Your Inner Child*. Madewith-lemons.co. https://madewithlemons.co/connect-with-your-inner-child/

Segers, K. (2022, July 28). *Inner Child Healing Therapy – A journey to Healing Your Inner Child - Awaken Inner Sense*. Awakeninnersense.com. https://awaken-innersense.com/inner-child-healing-therapy/

Self Forgiveness Is Essential For Healing. (n.d.). WellBeingAlignment. https://www.wellbeingalignment.com/self-forgiveness.html

Stacey. (2021, March 7). *An Introduction to Reparenting*. Maria Shriver. https://mariashriver.com/an-introduction-to-reparenting/

Stonecipher, B. (2016, July 14). *The Healing Power of Self-Forgiveness*. Richmond-magazine.com. https://richmondmagazine.com/the-healing-power-of-self-forgiveness/

Tewari, A. (2022, October 14). *111 Self-Care Affirmations for Inner Child, Peace, and Gratitude*. Gratitude - the Life Blog. https://blog.gratefulness.me/self-care-affirmations/amp/

Thalia. (2022, June 13). *How To Embrace Your Inner Child and Find Joy*. Notes by Thalia; Notes By Thalia. https://notesbythalia.com/embrace-your-inner-child-and-find-joy/

Trust Issues That Arise from Childhood Trauma. (2019, September 3). Psych Central. https://psychcentral.com/blog/psychology-self/2019/09/trust-issues#1

Turecki, J. (n.d.). *5 Reasons Why Maintaining a Healthy Relationship with Yourself Is Important*. JILLIAN TURECKI. https://www.jillianturecki.com/blog/why-maintaining-a-healthy-relationship-with-yourself-is-important

VIBGYOR Group of Schools. (2018). *5 Lessons You Can Learn From the Spirit of Childhood - VIBGYOR's Reading corner*. VIBGYOR's Reading Corner. https://www.vibgyorhigh.com/blog/2017/12/5-lessons-you-can-learn-from-the-spirit-of-childhood.html/amp

Warden, M. (2020, July 31). *You Must Let Go of Your False Self*. MichaelWarden. https://www.michaelwarden.com/post/you-must-let-go-of-your-false-self

Watson, K. (2014, September 14). *Creativity: 7 Ways To Connect With Your Inner Child*. Www.linkedin.com. https://www.linkedin.com/pulse/20140916123452-2807775-creativity-7-ways-to-connect-with-your-inner-child

Weatherhead, E. (2022, July 26). *Five Healing Ways to Re-Parent Your Inner Child*. Www.kmatherapy.com. https://www.kmatherapy.com/blog/inner-child-healing

Weber, J. P. (2015, July 15). *When Your "Inner Child" Hijacks Your Adult Relationships | Psychology Today*. Www.psychologytoday.com. https://www.psychologytoday.com/us/blog/having-sex-wanting-intimacy/201507/when-your-inner-child-hijacks-your-adult-relationships?amp

Webster, B. (2021, February 24). *Inner Child Healing Exercises: Validate and Differentiate*. Bethany Webster. https://www.bethanywebster.com/blog/inner-child-healing-exercises/

Weingus, L. (2022, May 17). *45 Journaling Prompts to Help Heal Your Inner Child and Unleash Joy*. Silk + Sonder. https://www.silkandsonder.com/blogs/news/inner-child-journal-prompts

What is Reparenting and How to Begin. (2019, July 2). The Holistic Psychologist. https://theholisticpsychologist.com/what-is-reparenting-and-how-to-begin

White, T. (2018, June 22). *Introjection and the integrated Adult*. Www.tony-White.com. https://www.tony-white.com/introjection-and-the-integrated-adult/

Printed in Great Britain
by Amazon

22130530R00074